ADVANCE PRAISE

"Every business owner struggles with issues around their business, especially surrounding the emotional side. Why do you do the work you do? What purpose does it serve? How can you get more fulfillment out of your business? Nick has explored these issues in depth and has some really interesting answers."

—CAMERON HEROLD, FOUNDER OF THE COO ALLIANCE, AND AUTHOR OF *DOUBLE DOUBLE* AND *MEETINGS SUCK*

"You are just as likely to solve a problem by being unconventional and determined as by being brilliant. That's my experience, and Exactly Where You Want to Be takes your hand and guides the business owner, making sure you embrace your misfit determination to have fun and make a profit. Read it."

—SIR JAMES DYSON OM CBE FRS FRENG, INVENTOR, INDUSTRIAL DESIGNER AND FOUNDER OF THE DYSON COMPANY

EXACTLY WHERE YOU WANT TO BE

EXACTLY WHERE YOU WANT TO BE

A BUSINESS OWNER'S GUIDE TO PASSION, PROFIT AND HAPPINESS

NICK LEIGHTON

LIONCREST
PUBLISHING

EXACTLY WHERE YOU WANT TO BE

A Business Owner's Guide to Passion, Profit and Happiness

ISBN   978-1-61961-790-2 *Paperback*

978-1-61961-791-9 *Ebook*

For my amazing wife, Tara. Wherever she
is, that's exactly where I want to be.

CONTENTS

———

PART I: WHERE DO *YOU* WANT TO BE?

    Challenges of business ownership • Reasons for starting
    or owning a business • The value of business ownership
    • Impact of small businesses on the economy • Finding
    your passion • Aligning your values with your passion

    The value of aligning your personal and professional
    visions • Determining your personal vision • Creating
    your personal vision statement • Honing the entrepre-
    neurial mindset

    Determining your business vision • Creating your busi-
    ness vision statement (and how to keep it relevant!) •
    Making sure your business vision fits with *your* business
    • How to determine your core values and guiding princi-
    ples • Establishing your critical success factors • Setting
    objectives and goals

PART II: THE TEN ROADS

ACKNOWLEDGMENTS

———

Running a business should be fun and so should writing a book. In this case, it was super fun, and that is due to a lot of people.

My mother, Alison, fueled my desire to write. I received a handwritten letter from her every day during my first lonely year of boarding school when I was about ten. That was unconditional love—and doubly appreciated since she is just as dyslexic as I am.

Whatever wisdom I have gained throughout my life has come from many areas and institutions of academics, working for passionate people, and running my own businesses. The teams who have been part of the companies I have owned, as well as the customers we have serviced, have pushed me daily and led to many of the realizations recorded here.

This book would not have come into fruition if it wasn't for the true professionals that made it possible. In particular, I must thank Tucker Max, Julie Arends, Mark Chait, and Chas Hoppe, all of whom have been amazing.

There are some key contributors to this book. These are all amazing, inspiring entrepreneurs who run awesome businesses. Thank you to George Jurica, Melissa Rigler, Torrey Tayenaka, Brian Olson, Crystal Williams, Allan Stone, Steve Peirce, Ed Simons, Gary Arch, Michael Haag, and Jason Quinn. Thank you for your willingness to share your story, and thank you for all the energy you give to your teams and customers—each of you give so much every day.

Another advisor who has shared his wisdom with me over the years deserves special thanks. Uncle Jeffrey is a self-made serial entrepreneur with the ability to break down complex issues, listen intently, and quickly provide astute observations that have driven me to think more clearly and remember solutions over the years. His stories are also awesome. Uncle Jeff, I hope you can hear some of your own advice in this book.

My *why* is simple. My wife, Tara, has inspired me every day since I met her. It is with deep love that I do more every day because of her. Our kids, Sophie and Ethan, make me laugh every day and bring me endless passion and happiness.

I wish everyone could have such a great team around them. Thank you to all.

INTRODUCTION

EXACTLY WHERE I
WANTED TO BE

———

We were being hijacked.

Moments before, everything was fine. Now, our team sat helplessly as the pilots of our helicopter gestured out the windows at the two fighter jets intercepting us.

How did I end up in this mess? Well, let me take you back in time.

I lived in Dubai in the United Arab Emirates, where I owned a marketing company called NettResults.[1] As part of our business, we did a lot of pro bono work for the

---

1   http://www.nettresults.com

United Nations, specifically for their World Food Program, one of the largest charities in the world. Our job provided global visibility and boosted donations for their school lunch initiative.

On the fateful day of our hijacking, we were flying through Pakistan on a humanitarian aid mission with a team of twenty international journalists. After meeting with some of the country's leaders and dignitaries, we set out in our old Russian helicopter to the Cashmere region, devastated by an earthquake the year before. There, we would deliver food to the poorest groups in the region and help guide the press through the UN-led relief efforts already underway.

At first, none of us noticed the in-progress hijacking. However, as I sat in the well-worn cabin, bags of corn at my feet, I realized the mountains were on the wrong side of the chopper.

"What's going on?" I asked one of the pilots.

"We're being hijacked," he said in a thick Russian accent. "These two fighter jets you can see on the side of us are dictating where we go."

We all agreed it was a good idea to follow the fighter jets' instructions. On my part, a sense of guilt crept in. Here

I was, tasked with looking after the welfare of twenty journalists from around the world, and I was about to get them kidnapped—or worse, killed.

I could already see the headlines.

Eventually, we were instructed to land in a nearby school field, albeit one surrounded by guards with machine guns. Our captors then shuffled us into the back of a truck, and off we went to destinations unknown.

Not too far away, we ended up at a makeshift camp set up to house the many families who had lost their homes in the quake.

No one mistreated or manhandled us—outside of the initial hijacking, that is. They even offered us tea and cookies as we walked around, took pictures, and spoke with some of the displaced people living there.

This was a relief, as any overtly aggressive or even violent behavior would have been met with a great deal of confusion. You see, no one else in our group outside of the pilots and myself knew what was going on. The rest of the journalists all thought we were simply on a small detour from our itinerary.

In a way, that was true enough. The hijackers managing the camp had learned we were headed to the area with a team of journalists. In a move of aggressive PR, they wanted to showcase their own humanitarian efforts for the world to see.

Naturally, there were limits to what we were allowed to observe. If any of us strayed too far beyond the main camp-site, we were pushed back. We were there to observe the aid our hijackers were providing and nothing more. After about an hour, we got back on the truck, returned to our helicopter, and were carried on our way.

I should have been terrified throughout this ordeal, but I wasn't. I was exactly where I wanted to be.

Sure, I may have been in some danger, but I was doing what I loved, all while working with international journalists in an international setting. I believed in the United Nations' aid work, and I knew our efforts would have great results. I was completely absorbed in the moment—and I was even having fun.

EXACTLY WHERE YOU WANT TO BE

To me, the story of my hijacking is a lot like business ownership. It may seem scary to other people, but we business owners believe in what we're doing. Even more, we are confident that our efforts *matter*.

Being a business owner is about doing your own thing. It's about setting out on a mission that doesn't feel like a chore, a mission that feels right for the life you want to live. It's about doing what you want to be doing. It's about being where you want to be.

According to research from Penn State University, business owners are famously endowed with a bias toward optimism.[2] This is doubly true for serial entrepreneurs, who see new situations as an opportunity to hit a home run.

That said, the business owner's life is often stressful. The long hours, tight deadlines, and inevitable setbacks make it feel like it's impossible to stay above water.

Of course, you know this already. That's why you're reading this book.

You know being in business for yourself is one of the most important things you will ever do. You also know, and

---

2   Chyi-lyi (Kathleen) Liang & Paul Dunn. "Entrepreneurial Characteristics, Optimism, Pessimism, and Realism—Correlation or Collision?" *Journal of Business and Entrepreneurship* 22, no.1 (March 2010): 1–22.

have no doubt experienced, that business ownership will present you with challenges you never dreamed of.

This book is designed to get you where you want to be. It's about helping you get on track and remembering why you do what you do in the first place.

Above all, it's about creating a life filled with a sense of fun and adventure.

WHERE I CAME FROM

To help you understand why I've written this book, let me tell you a little about me.

My mother and father have been married seven times, but never to each other. They met at a party in London in the early seventies, and within a short amount of time, they decided to get in a car together and drive south. Unfortunately, you can't head south from London for long before you reach the English Channel.

Not wanting to let a body of water stand in their way, my parents hopped on a boat, landed in France, made their way down to the Mediterranean, and hopped on another boat to Greece—specifically to a small island called Spetses, where I spent the first few years of my life.

From these origins, it's not hard to see where I get my sense of adventure. I may have been a child of the Western world, but I was the product of two passionate explorers living on a small island that imported fresh water twice a week by boat.

Before I caused too many problems on that small Greek island, I moved back to my parents' homeland in the United Kingdom, where I attended boarding school and completed my primary schooling. As an undergraduate, I studied in Leicester, the UK, and on exchange in North Carolina; I eventually traveled across the United States, and ended up in California. After a time, I headed back to the United Kingdom where I earned my MBA.

At first, I worked for a small recycling company. When a global tech company scooped me up, my passion for international travel resurged. First, they moved me to Paris, France, and then to Prague, in the Czech Republic. Eventually, I ended up in Dubai, United Arab Emirates, had my little helicopter hijacking adventure, and then I relocated to Southern California.

In all, I've either lived or worked in both North and South America, Europe, the Middle East, Africa, and Asia. I can't say every stop was planned, but it was always exactly where I wanted to be.

WHERE I AM TODAY

Today, I run three businesses.

The first is an international marketing agency called NettResults,[3] where I work for amazing brands with a fantastic group of people. There, my day-to-day interaction is relatively small, but I get to do what I love: talking to clients and managing campaigns.

The second is a project management company I cofounded with my wife, called The inScope Group.[4] There, my wife masterfully navigates the day-to-day needs of running the business and keeps very complex multimillion-dollar projects on time, on budget, and within scope.

The bulk of my work is focused at my third business, where I coach business owners one-on-one to help make their vision a reality and achieve their dreams both in their personal and professional lives. Meeting every two weeks or so, my clients and I focus on building strategic plans for improving the day-to-day operations of their businesses— much like you and I will do together throughout this book.

I also run peer advisory boards, which I like to say is like ‘having your own board of directors, but without having

3   http://nettresultsllc.com

4   http://inscopegroup.com

to pay for the *other* board of directors. These boards are made up of local business owners working in a variety of industries. It doesn't matter what business each is in; all business owners face the same opportunities and challenges. Our job is to create an environment where they can be open and transparent about their business so we can give them honest feedback.

Why do I work so closely with other business owners to help them succeed? As I will explain in the first chapter, it's lonely at the top, and it's hard to find others who have gone through the same things you have. Our peer advisory boards are full of amazing people with amazing experiences. They are happy to help others steer clear of the many landmines on the road to business ownership by offering open dialogue, continued education, and honest accountability.

To me, there's nothing better than seeing people reach their "champagne moments," those irreplaceable instances in every business owner's life where they've snatched victory, often against all odds. I'll explain everything this entails later, but for now, I'll say it is a privilege to help others make these moments a reality.

HOW TO READ THIS BOOK

Enough about me. Let's talk about you and how both you and your business can benefit from this book.

Part I is a must-read. After all, to build your business, you must first start with a stable foundation. It doesn't matter if you're just getting started or looking to tune up your current enterprise. Make sure you read these chapters and do the exercises included within.

From there, the journey is up to you. I used to love reading those choose-your-own-adventure books, and I want you to think about this book in a similar way.

At this point, I should mention that you're going to hear a lot about me and the adventures that got me where I wanted to be—whether being hijacked in Pakistan, running into burning buildings, or dashing about on a high-speed chase on the streets of Russia. Just so you don't think this is all about me, you're also going to hear from a lot of my clients as they learned to recognize and master the myriad challenges confronting their own businesses.

Every chapter builds off the last in an order that makes sense to me. However, some areas you may have more experience in than others, some may not apply to you, and some may have more urgency. If that means jumping from Chapter 9 back to Chapter 5 and then up to 10, then so be it. Feel free to mix and match however you want.

Each chapter can be read in fifteen minutes and is chock-full of practical advice and real-world tips you can use. If you get to the end of any chapter and don't think it was worth ten times the cost of this book, then throw it in the trash immediately. Life is too short to keep reading on. Then, email me, tell me which chapter sucks, and I will suggest some excellent alternative resources.

Perhaps you find the book useful overall, but find certain sections of the book so wrong or off base that you want to pull your hair out. My advice: It's totally okay to disagree with me, so why not hang onto your hair a little while longer? The tips and strategies have worked wonders for me and my businesses, as well as for the business leaders I've coached, but that doesn't mean there aren't other ways of going about things.

Finally, if you *really* want to have fun, I suggest you get as active as possible:

- Write notes all over the book (unless you have a digital copy, in which case I'd recommend your app's annotation feature).

- Set aside the time to try every exercise I've included. Seriously, there's no better way of learning than by doing.
- Check out the book's dedicated resources site—filled with content for every chapter—where you can grab templates and share some of your fun and passion with others.[5]

Sound good? Great! Let's get started.

---

5   Each chapter will give you a specific page to turn to, but if you want to check out the site right now, it's http://exactlywhereyouwanttobe.com

PART I

WHERE DO *YOU* WANT TO BE?

When I work with business owners, the first thing I ask is, "Why are you in business?" Often, much to their own surprise, they don't have a good answer.

I've found most people get into business for two reasons:

1. They decided to.
2. They were forced to.

Sure, there's usually more to the story. Perhaps they couldn't find a job and decided to strike out on their own. Perhaps they took over after the previous owner decided to retire. Whatever the case may be, it usually boils down to choice or circumstance.

In the following chapters, you will learn how to identify your purpose. You may know why you got started, but I challenge you to set a new vision for your future.

To identify your purpose, we'll cover the who, the what, and the why of successful business ownership. By understanding yourself, your business, and your reason for being, you establish a mindset and a vision that will carry over into everything you do, from big-picture strategies to day-to-day routines.

Before you turn the page, go ahead and ask yourself the following questions:

- Who are you?
- What are you doing?
- Why are you doing it?

Not sure yet? Let's see if the following chapters can help spark an idea.

CHAPTER 1

WHY ARE YOU IN THE BUSINESS THAT YOU'RE IN?

The way to get started is to quit talking and begin doing.

—WALT DISNEY

Let's face it: owning a company is a pain. You've no doubt experienced sleepless nights, staring at the ceiling and wondering how you're going to pay your team members, your rent, your taxes, and yourself.

Never mind the money. What about the stress? At one point or another, your team members, partners, and suppliers—even your customers—will let you down, and you will work so hard you forget to eat right and exercise.

On top of all that, hardly anyone understands what you're doing. Your parents, life partner, kids, family, friends, and anyone else you hold in high regard might rightfully decide you've gone mad.

It's not a happy reality, but the truth is business owners often suffer considerable frustration in their personal lives—losing friends, alienating family members, and even damaging or losing their marriages.

With all these factors coming at you, it's only fair to ask: Why do you want to own your own company?

THE TRUTH ABOUT STARTING A BUSINESS

When you start your own business, there is no guarantee of success. In fact, it's easy to look at the numbers and see the deck isn't stacked in your favor.

Per the latest stats, 25 percent of all businesses fail in the first year, and 55 percent fail in the first five years. After ten years, only 29 percent of businesses are still in operation.[6]

---

6   *Entrepreneur Weekly*. "Startup Business Failure Rate by Industry." Small Business Development Center, Bradley University, University of Tennessee Research. http://www.statisticbrain.com/startup-failure-by-industry. Accessed July 27, 2013.

A NEW DAWN, A NEW BUSINESS

Despite the odds, business owners are an optimistic and enthusiastic lot. While different studies vary in their findings, thousands of new businesses pop up every day.

For instance, the United States alone saw 600,000 new businesses in 2011.[7] Here's a look at the average annual numbers of new businesses around the world:

- The United Kingdom: 430,000
- Hong Kong, China: 148,000
- France: 132,000
- Australia: 94,000

Globally, that's over three new companies every thirty seconds.

These numbers speak to a boundless optimism, but in fact, it gets better. For every business owner who successfully launches a new business, countless more are considering it or preparing to do so.

---

7 According to the US Census Bureau, approximately 543,000 new businesses get started each month: https://www.census.gov/topics/business/small-business.html

SMALL BUSINESSES ARE BIG BUSINESS

All these new businesses add up. In fact, they're a major driving force of the economy.

According to surveys in 2015 by the *Global Entrepreneurship Monitor*, more than 12 percent of US adults reported starting a business or running new businesses, which is up from 8 percent in 2010.[8]

Of these, we can break them down into three categories:

1. Solopreneurs (non-employers)
2. Small businesses
3. Large businesses (five hundred or more employees)

According to 2011 data from the US Small Business Administration, there were 28.2 million small businesses and fewer than 20,000 large businesses (firms with 500 employees or more). Of those roughly 28 million small businesses, three-quarters were run by solopreneurs—a number that has continued to rise in recent years.[9]

---

8   Global Entrepreneurship Monitor 2015 United States Report: http://www. gemconsortium.org/country-profile/122

9   "Frequently Asked Questions." Small Business Administration Office of Advocacy. https://www.sba.gov/sites/default/files/FAQ_March_2014_0.pdf

With small businesses far outnumbering large businesses, and with solopreneurs taking up the largest slice of the small business pie, we can say without a doubt that in the United States, small business is *big* business. America's economy depends on the optimism and energy of its business owners.

Don't believe me? Look at these numbers. Small businesses:

- Make up 99.7 percent of the US employer firms
- Consist of 64 percent of net new private sector jobs
- Make up 42.9 percent of private sector payroll[10]

Small businesses also account for 43 percent of all employment in the tech industry and 98 percent of US exports. In fact, an impressive 33 percent of exports measured by value come from small businesses.

WHY DO ENTREPRENEURS GO INTO BUSINESS?

I've worked with business owners across America, Europe, the Middle East, Africa, and Asia. When I ask why they're in business for themselves, they all say the same thing: they enjoy the freedom it affords them.

10 US Census Bureau, SUSB, CPS; International Trade Administration; Bureau of Labor Statistics, BED; Advocacy-funded research, Small Business GDP: Update 2002-2010: www.sba.gov/advocacy/7540/42371. For the latest employment statistics, see Advocacy's quarterly reports at www.sba.gov/advocacy/10871.

But is this true? Are business owners more free?

By the number of hours worked, not really. According to research from Wells Fargo, business owners work an average of fifty-two hours a week with over half working at least six days a week.

These numbers reflect the business owners I coach, who usually work between forty and fifty hours a week. When asked how many hours they would *like* to work, half would prefer to work about twenty hours a week, while the other half wants to double their efforts.

Clearly, freedom can't be defined by hours worked alone. Perhaps it's more a matter of better work/life balance—or what I like to call work/life integration. After all, with today's personal communication devices, such as phones and tablets, business owners can take care of business anywhere. And I love a sandy beach or foreign café for my office.

Perhaps freedom is better defined by one's ability to call the shots. I know I can relate. When a mentor asked me, "Why do you want to do this?" I realized there was only one right answer: because I want to.

COMMON REASONS FOR STARTING A COMPANY

Truly, nothing beats that feeling of self-determination. Not only do business owners enjoy calling the shots, they also enjoy other benefits of being their own boss, such as:

- Control over their own destiny
- Work/life balance
- The ability to choose the people they work with
- Greater risk but also greater reward
- The personal challenge
- The chance to follow their passion
- The freedom to work faster
- Connecting with clients on a deeper level
- Giving back to the community
- Pride in building something

These are all good reasons for starting a business. However, there are two others: the desire for easy money and the quest for personal happiness.

If you started a business for either of these reasons, I hope you'll commit to reading the following pages and get ready to challenge yourself. Don't worry, you can have both money and happiness. They are not mutually exclusive, and in this book, you're going to learn how to make sure of it.

However, before you read on to learn how it's done, let's get one point clear: your business won't bring you these things. *You* will bring them to your business.

IT'S LONELY AT THE TOP

Here's one thing I can guarantee you, a strong feeling I experienced in my own independent start-ups, and what I've heard echoed by countless other business owners throughout my career: you will feel alone—very, very alone.

When you're in business for yourself, you'll know in no uncertain terms that the buck stops with you.

As an employee, particularly in a large company, I could leave work for the day with various problems and challenges unresolved. By the next morning, many of them would have solved themselves.

What a great—dare I say, glorious—feeling that was, knowing everything would always work out. If I had a problem with my computer, I'd call tech support. If I had a problem with people, I'd call HR. If I had a problem with a customer or supplier, I'd call my boss.

None of that exists when you own your own business, at least, not unless you're paying for outside help.

WHO DELIVERS THE GOODS?

When you work for someone else, it's easy to get frustrated by your employer's inefficiencies: the politics, the wasted time, the team members with conflicts of interest, the team members who show up and check out, etc.

Business owners, on the other hand, control their own destiny. Especially when you're starting out, if you want something done, you do it yourself.

It's fine to carry on this way for a while, but most business owners never get past this hurdle. Eventually, you'll have to transition from relying on your ingenuity alone to relying on others to carry out your vision.

I get it. It's hard to let go. The longer you go at it alone, the more anecdotal evidence you amass to reinforce the idea that you must be involved in everything. It's easy to fall into this trap, but if you want to find true success as a business owner, you must trust others to deliver.

PUT YOUR ENERGY WHERE
YOU'RE MOST VALUABLE

Most business owners are very adaptive at problem solving. If you need something done, then go ask a business owner. Even if we don't know what to do and don't have much time to do it, we'll find a way to get it done.

I once had the pleasure of listening to Paul Orfalea, founder of Kinko's (now FedEx Offices). During the talk, Orfalea talked about how, despite his lack of technical skills, when one of his photocopiers stopped working, he took it upon himself to figure out how to get it back up and running.

Soon, he realized if he could figure things out like this, then others in his organization could—and should—too. After all, as the CEO, he had bigger problems to solve. Soon, he learned how to become unavailable, building the spirit of total personal service into the Kinko's business model.

This is one of the best examples I've seen of successfully building a company that does not rely on the time and expertise of its founder, though it relied on him to provide clarity of purpose. For your own success and happiness, make sure you're not the only person needed to make the shop run.

We'll talk about recruitment later, but if you come across a team member or supplier that doesn't need constant explanation to get a job done, then nurture that relationship. Team members like these are the business owner's most valuable tool.

FROM DISSATISFACTION TO SATISFACTION

Here's the first rule to succeeding as a business owner: you should love what you do.

I know, passion seems obvious, but sometimes the obvious things are the most important to keep in mind. If you aren't passionate about what you do, then you should quit doing it.

Often, the problem isn't a lack of passion, but rather a surplus. Unfortunately, this passion overload doesn't always translate to business success, as these business owners often have trouble keeping their eyes on the big picture. More on that later.

PASSION PLAYS

As the founder of your business, you had better have more passion than the people buying from you. If nothing else, it's the best way to nurture passionate team members who are dedicated to your brand.

Here's an example. One of my favorite California restaurants is called Playground DTSA,[11] which stands for "Downtown Santa Anna." The Playground brand rose from humble beginnings, eventually competing on the show *The Great Food Truck Race*. From there, founder

11   http://www.playgroundtsa.com/

Jason Quinn and his team's venture grew from a popular food truck to a full-service restaurant.

It's not just the food that makes the Playground so special. Quinn and his team are committed to their culinary journey, even sharing matching tattoos that epitomize the passion, view, and branding of the Playground.

My question for you is this: How many people on your team would be passionate enough to tattoo your brand on their bodies?

HOW TO FIND YOUR PASSION

As nineteenth-century British Prime Minister Benjamin Disraeli once said, "Man is only great when he acts from passion." The only way to be a truly inspiring leader is to be obsessed with what you do.

If you don't know what your passion is, then you haven't found one, or you haven't given it enough thought. In any case, here are three things to consider:

1. Think back to what resonated with you early in your life. Most passions strike people at an early age. Anyone can be clever, but the most successful students are the ones who study what they love.

2. Put together a vision board or a group of pictures that means something to you. Not the scrapbooking type? Not to worry: you can achieve the same goal on Pinterest.

3. Think of the people around you, now or in the past, who have influenced you. Whether they're alive or dead, whether you know them or merely know of them, identify the ones who inspire and empower you to act.

Once you've tried out these strategies, ask yourself: How does your passion drive the work you do? If it doesn't, what can you do to bring that passion to the forefront?

↳ especially if you're teetering out on a project.

ALIGNING YOUR VALUES WITH YOUR PASSIONS

As every sensible businessperson will tell you (I try to avoid sensible), passion alone is not going to make a successful business. While the rest of this book will help you channel your passion into profit and happiness, for now, I will simply stress that your business is only going to succeed if you're filling a desperate need or solving an urgent problem.

To make your passion work *for* you, make sure it aligns with your values, which for our purposes can be defined as your principles or standards of behavior.

Trusting your judgment is important to finding happiness in life. If you don't trust your judgment or choose to ignore it, you could end up like the high-level clean energy-minded geologist working in an oil refinery: unhappy, insecure, and at the mercy of your employer.

SOME QUESTIONS BEFORE MOVING ON

Before we move on to the next chapter, take a moment to think about these things for yourself. You should find the answers to be quite revealing.

- What about your business makes you willing to endure the pain that comes with it?
- Why are you in the business you're in?
- Why did you launch the business?
- Do you still feel the same way about your business?

Stop, stop, stop! If you're still reading without taking pause, then you're missing the point. Stop and think about each of these questions. You want the value, right?

Okay, now that you've had a moment to think, let's push forward with the rest of the questions.

- How did you become involved in your business? Was it by choice or by chance?

- Are other family members involved in your business?
- What do you like about your business?
- What don't you like about your business?
- Do you have a vision for your business?
- Why would I do business with you versus your competitor?
- What keeps you awake at night?

NOW FOR SOME FUN

At the end of each chapter in this book, you'll find a fun prompt based on what you just read. You could respond to this on your own or with a colleague, but it would be doubly fun if you shared your response in an open forum.

On the book's website,[12] you'll find a webpage dedicated to each chapter. Along with tools and templates, each will include an open forum to share and have fun with other business owners.

Here's the prompt for this chapter:

Just like Playground DTSA and their employee tattoos, we show passion in many ways. What's the biggest passion you've witnessed at your or another business?

Once you've given it some thought, share here:

http://exactlywhereyouwanttobe.com/why

---

12   http://exactlywhereyouwanttobe.com

CHAPTER 2

WHO ARE YOU?

———

*If you don't love something, you're not
going to go the extra mile, work the extra
weekend, challenge the status quo as much.*

—STEVE JOBS

I was visiting a cousin who was busy planning her wedding reception. The whole affair was a big to-do, with guests coming from the other side of the world to attend.

Countless details had to be arranged, including venue, valet parking, and signature drinks for the martini bar. Two weeks before the event, I watched in awe as my cousin stood in the center of all this chaos and masterfully orchestrated every little detail.

I knew she'd been dreaming about this moment since she was a little girl. Yet, as the event grew increasingly complex and more people got involved, I couldn't imagine how she managed it all. So, I asked her.

"It's easy," she replied. "I have a theme no one else knows: English summer garden. When I'm presented with three choices for flowers, table settings, videography style, the valet boys' clothing, or the names of martinis, I ask myself which one is closest to my theme."

I found her answer brilliant. My cousin showed not only a tremendous personal vision with her answer, but also a deep understanding of who she was.

Even more, she was demonstrating a core principle of business ownership. Whether in weddings or in business, you can't create passion, profit, and happiness unless you know who you are.

ALIGNING YOUR VISIONS

As the story of my cousin demonstrates, every decision is easy to make when you know who you are and what you want. In business, knowing these things can help you decide what you should achieve, how to travel the road to success, and how to have fun along the way.

In his book, *Strategic Business Leadership*, a favorite of The Alternative Board, author Alan Fishman says being a business owner is like riding a bicycle. The front wheel represents your personal vision—who you are, what you want, and what's important to you. The back wheel represents your company, which brings you revenue, remuneration, and all the other benefits.

If your front wheel and your back wheel—in other words, your personal and business visions—are aligned, then life is good. It's like you're cycling downhill with the wind at your back. If your wheels aren't aligned, well, you get the picture.

HOW DO YOU GREET THE DAY?

When you wake up every morning, you should be inspired by your business. It should motivate you, drive you, and grow your passion.

I'm sure you know people like this, those wonderfully exuberant types who attack every day with remarkable vigor. Whether they're in business for themselves or not, I'm willing to bet their personal and professional visions are aligned.

WHAT IS YOUR PERSONAL VISION?

Before you can set a professional vision, you first need to have a personal vision.

If you already have your personal vision and repeat it to yourself every day, then great. You're golden.

However, if you don't have a personal vision, there's no need to worry. You're right there with most of the population.

The question now is simple: How are you going to get it?

YOUR VERY OWN VISION QUEST

To have a personal vision, you must know yourself. I know, this is easier said than done. After all, self-actualization is Maslow's highest level, and some people spend most of their lives trying to know their true selves.

I'm not going to deprive you of that privilege. However, for our journey in this book, there is a speedier method to knowing yourself that should work just fine.

It all boils down to the following fifteen questions. Go ahead and give them a look, and then write down some short responses for each—whatever feels good to you. I'll warn you: the first question is going to be the hardest.

#1: WHAT IS YOUR "WHY?"

What do you desire? Why do you do what you do? What's important to you? If you could use one word to capture why you are the way you are, what would it be?

#2: WHAT BUSINESS AREAS GIVE YOU THE MOST PLEASURE?

How can you be involved in your business in a way that fills you with passion and helps you excel? For example, some of my clients have said they like creating new processes, selling to large accounts, mentoring family members, or developing strategic plans or alliances.

#3: WHAT ACTIVITIES DO YOU WANT TO DELEGATE?

What business activities are you currently doing that you would prefer not to do? For instance, some business owners want to delegate things like bookkeeping, administration, selling, or HR.

#4: WHAT ARE YOUR WORK TIME COMMITMENTS?

How much time do you want to spend working during a typical week? Do you want to work fifty hours a week, three days a week, or only mornings?

#5: HOW MUCH VACATION TIME DO YOU WANT?

Do you want to take two to four weeks off a year or two to four weeks off a quarter? Do you want to take a whole month off during the summer? Do you need ten days off a year? Do you just need the occasional long weekend? Do you want to be an international traveler during your vacation time with no contact from work whatsoever?

#6: WHAT IS YOUR DESIRED ANNUAL COMPENSATION?

What is the total annual compensation package that will give you and your family the financial freedom you want? Maybe it's a $250K annual salary with a company car, tax advantages for your home office, and a million frequent flyer miles. Some business owners want to make half a million dollars a year, while others are happy with much less.

#7: WHAT ARE YOUR INTANGIBLE REWARDS?

Outside of money, why are you in business? Maybe you want to have a leading company in the industry, cultivate political influence, or create high-paying jobs for your team members.

#8: WHAT ARE YOUR SPIRITUAL BELIEFS?

What spiritual beliefs motivate you and bring happiness to your personal life? Some people want to be active members of their religious congregation. Others simply don't want to work on the Sabbath or on other religious days.

In fact, your spiritual days don't have to be religious holidays. Some business owners say never work on President's Day or Halloween. Whatever your belief system is, it's important to determine how it impacts your work.

#9: WHAT NONBUSINESS ACTIVITIES BRING YOU PEACEFULNESS OR CONTENTMENT?

Here, I'm referring mostly to hobbies or other leisure activities. It could be anything—family time, hiking, reading, going to the theater, studying, skiing, sailing, etc.

#10: WHAT KINDS OF PERSONAL ACHIEVEMENTS BRING YOU FULFILLMENT?

Do you want to go back to school and earn an MBA or another certification? Do you want to write a book? What makes you proud?

#11: WHAT ARE YOUR HUMANITARIAN INTERESTS?

How do you like giving back to your community? Perhaps it's hiring vets, volunteering at a children's hospital, or creating a charitable trust. Many business owners can answer this question immediately, though plenty of others aren't so sure.

#12: WHAT FAMILY INVOLVEMENT IS IMPORTANT TO YOU?

Do you need to be home for dinner five nights a week? Are Sunday barbecues essential to your happiness? Do you want to read your children bedtime stories every evening? What about having the whole family over for your birthday?

#13: WHAT LEVEL OF HEALTH, NUTRITION, AND ACTIVITY MAKES YOU FEEL GOOD?

Everyone has different personal benchmarks. These could include proper diet and eating habits, exercising, meeting daily step counts, or looking after your body in some way.

#14: WHAT ARE YOUR RETIREMENT PLANS?

Some business owners have firm retirement plans, while others prefer to remain involved in their business in some capacity. Some people never want to retire, while others want to retain an ownership interest but let other people do all the work.

#15: WHAT IS YOUR EXIT STRATEGY?

Are you going to sell your business, give it to family members, or let someone else take over while you retain ownership? Do you want to sell to your team members or to an outside buyer?

If you do want to sell your business, what is the minimum value at which you're willing to sell? What's your timeline for selling? For example, do you want to sell the business before you're sixty for a minimum of $2 million?

THE PERSONAL VISION STATEMENT

Now that you've answered these fifteen questions, it's time to craft your personal vision statement. A short bullet list under a hundred words should be fine. Try this one as an example:

· Maintain controlling interest in my business and grow sales while reducing my workload, so I do not have to work on Fridays.

- Take $450K annual income from my business to maintain my current lifestyle.
- Take at least one week off a quarter. Of those, two weeks should involve international travel.
- Only perform activities in the business I enjoy, including selling to major clients and handling media relations.
- Develop the business so it will be sellable to a third party for $3 million within ten years.
- Make someone's day every single day.
- Be part of the business owner success story.

FINISH THIS BEFORE MOVING ON

Stop right here. Do you have your personal vision yet? If not, you have one of two options:

1. Take mine from the previous section, change a few words, and add your own name.
2. Go back to those fifteen questions and spend the next thirty minutes or so on this exercise. I know, this one's a bit harder, but I promise you, it's more satisfying.

Go on. Don't skip ahead until you have a personal vision. Trust me, it's worth it.

THE GRASS IS ALWAYS GREENER

Now, it's time for a quick sanity check on your personal vision statement.

One of the reasons I love my job is, with all the hundreds of entrepreneurs and business owners I've worked with, all of their vision statements are optimistically inclined. See for yourself: the grass is always greener through the entrepreneur's eyes.

- In a flagging economy, mere mortals bemoan the fact they can't eat out as much, while entrepreneurs anticipate dining without reservations and enjoying longer happy hours.
- When unemployment rises, mere mortals say, "Bummer, now it's harder to find a job," while entrepreneurs say, "Great! Now it's easier to find good talent."
- If a key member leaves an organization, mere mortals worry about finding, onboarding, and training someone new, while entrepreneurs see a chance to restructure and grow more efficient.

Personally, I like the way Epictetus, the Greek philosopher who lived between 55 and 135 AD, said it: "It's not what happens to you, but how you react to it that matters." Epictetus would have gotten along great with my grandmother, who always insisted everything had a silver lining.

Here's my point: what makes the personal vision statement powerful is it has an uncanny ability to change your perspective for the better.

DREAM BIG. THINK BIG. BE BIG.

Now that you're armed with your personal vision, I want you to make an active, conscious effort to avoid thinking or speaking in negative terms.

This doesn't mean you should stop being sarcastic and start being overly nice to everyone. (Seriously, most of my best friends are sarcastic and think most people are stupid.) There are plenty of ways to keep your wit while maintaining a positive frame of mind. In the long run, your business will be better off for it.

I have yet to meet anyone who can't achieve what they set out to achieve. Think about it: it only took one suffragette to bring women's rights to the world, one dream to secure equal rights, one idea to drive every business revolution you have ever experienced.

Dream big. Think big. Be big.

Above all, if you want it, go for it.

THE PERSONAL VISION IN ACTION

Meet Charlotte, one of my former clients.

Charlotte is a smart, savvy, and highly successful entrepreneur who masterfully balances a successful company, a happy marriage, and two young daughters.

She used to work for a small insurance company. However, on a cycling holiday with some friends in Italy one year, she was inspired to forge her own path. On her return to California, she set up her own insurance business, built a stable of great clients, and managed to strike a good balance between business and family. Things were off to a great start.

When I met Charlotte several years later, she didn't have a minute to spare. She worked feverishly between school runs, worked late at night to make up for lost time, and even worked a few extra hours on the weekends. In effect, she had become an employee working for herself.

For many business owners, this is a familiar story.

As we worked through Charlotte's personal vision, I asked her when she had last been cycling. After hesitating for a moment, she laughed out loud and then admitted that her bicycle was hanging in the garage, untouched since that Italian vacation.

When she told me this, I followed up by asking what was most important to her. Can you guess what she said—and what she hadn't been doing for several years?

Fast-forward a few months. Charlotte has taken on her first team member, reduced her day-to-day workload, and is having her bike serviced ahead of her next cycling trip. Even better, her revenues have dramatically improved.

No doubt about it, having a personal vision matters.

MAKING IT WORK FOR YOU

So far, we've talked about all the reasons for owning a company and all the positive factors you can leverage for passion, profit, and happiness.

However, what about the business owners who don't have the luxury of choice? Plenty of people started their own business because they were pushed into it, because they lost their last job, or because they couldn't find other employment.

Whether business ownership was your choice or not, you can still make it work for you on your own terms. Even if you didn't choose this path, be conscious of why you're doing it and what you want out of it.

NOW FOR SOME FUN

Who are you? It's not just the members of The Who (Roger Daltrey, Pete Townshend, John Entwistle, and Keith Moon) who really wanna know. I, and plenty of other members of the business community, wanna know too.

I shared mine. Now it's time to share yours. What's your personal vision?

Once you've given it some thought, share here:

http://exactlywhereyouwanttobe.com/who

CHAPTER 3

WHAT IS YOUR VISION FOR YOUR BUSINESS?

———

Build your own dreams, or someone else will hire you to build theirs.

—FARRAH GREY

A business strategy is the engine that propels your organization forward, driving you to achieve your personal vision. Think of it as a starting point for mapping out what your company plans to do over the next three to five years.

Anyone can benefit from a well-thought-out business strategy. However, 99 percent of the business owners I speak to never got around to making one. If I'm being honest, the other 1 percent who have a strategy are no better, since they usually tuck those plans away in an office drawer somewhere and forget about them...forever.

What about you? What is your business strategy?

If you aren't sure, don't worry. Just keep reading.

Remember, a good vision doesn't come out of thin air. You must work at it. First, you set a vision, then you create objectives, and finally you develop key strategies and tactics to turn your vision into reality.

SETTING YOUR BUSINESS VISION

After the last chapter, vision should be second nature to you. You already did the hard part of figuring out your *personal* vision, so you're halfway there.

Here's the good news: while it took a whole fifteen questions to set your personal vision, you can craft your business vision in only eight.

Just as before, take a look at the following questions, consider your answers, and write a couple words down for each one.

#1: BUSINESS EXISTENCE PURPOSE

Why does your business exist for *you* beyond profit? There should be a reason beyond money that motivates you. Do you have a killer invention you want to take to the market? Do you dream of improving children's lives all over the world? Do you want to help others, or are you driven by something else?

#2: PRODUCTS AND SERVICES

What are your company's principal products and services? What principal products and services would you like in your company's future?

#3: CUSTOMERS

Who are your primary customers, clients, or users? Who would you like as your *future* primary customers, clients, or users?

#4: GEOGRAPHICAL AREAS

What geographical markets do you compete in? Where would you like to compete in the future?

#5: STAKEHOLDERS

Anyone who encounters your business is a stakeholder—including customers, team members, vendors, and investors. Is there a difference between how you treat your stakeholders and how *you want* to treat them?

#6: DISTRIBUTION CHANNELS

What are your company's principal outlets or distribution channels, including traditional brick-and-mortar and online? What other principal outlets or distribution channels would you like to be part of in the future?

#7: INDUSTRY LEADERSHIP

What level of leadership in your industry's professional community do you have? Who do you network with? Who is in your sphere of influence?

#8: COMPANY VALUES

What core values, beliefs, and principles are important to you for your company's future? The easiest ones that everyone tells me are honesty, integrity, and accountability. What's your desired company culture? For example, perhaps you want a workforce committed to superior customer service.

CRAFTING YOUR BUSINESS VISION STATEMENT

Now that you've written some notes down, it's time to write a short business vision statement. Just like your personal vision statement, it's best if you keep this to a short bullet list under a hundred words. Here's an example:

- Be an organization recognized for offering business owners the best advantage to business success.
- Cultivate clients who are North American business owners with the desire to take their business to the next level, while having fun.
- Have an enlightened, skilled, dynamic, and forward-thinking management team and outsource everything we can.
- Seamlessly bundle consulting and non-time-based products together to provide cost-effective solutions.
- Partner with best-in-class service professionals who are aligned with our organization's culture and objectives.
- Promote passion, profit, and happiness within our organization and with everyone we touch.

Now that you've read my example business vision, it's your turn to give it a try.

DOES THE VISION FIT?

Got your business vision all squared away? Great, now let's give it a look.

Here's the first question to ask yourself: Does your business vision epitomize your organization?

You don't want to make your vision so vague it could apply to any company. This may be an organizational statement, but it needs to reflect you, the leader, and your personal view of your business.

In other words, it should mean something to you. It should have your character.

To infuse your business vision with your own personal flair, you need to be in touch with your personal vision. In fact, your business vision should outlast every team member at your company—even you.

As we'll see later, very few organizations have teams that last as long as the company itself. According to the Bureau of Labor Statistics, as of January 2014, the median time wage and salary workers had been with their current employer was 4.6 years.

Even in the best companies, team members come and go. It's up to you as the owner to make, communicate, and keep your company culture alive. No one else will be around long enough to do this for you.

BUSINESS CULTURE AND GUIDING PRINCIPLES

Now that we've discussed why a strong business vision leads to a strong company, let's talk about culture. Why is it so important?

I'll start with the short answer: To translate your business vision into reality, I'm 99.99-percent sure that you'll need others to help you. If you're a one-person superpower, skip this section. No big deal.

CORE VALUES

Business culture is driven by guiding principles, also known as core values. If you did your homework and completed your business vision earlier, then you've already thought about your company values.

In life, the truth is we have an entire universe of values. Some of them are so primary, so important to us, we hold fast to them no matter how society changes, which elected officials come into power, or what new technologies transform our lives.

Just as you can't change someone's core values, you shouldn't change your company's guiding principles. After all, these values are the basic elements underlying our work, how we interact with others, and the strategies we employ to fulfill our mission. They are the practices we use—or should be using—every day and in everything we do.

Your business's core values help guide behavior and choice. Get them right, and your decision-making will be swift and focused. Get them wrong or leave them ambiguous, and you'll be constantly wondering how you got yourself into whatever new mess you've discovered.

THE BENEFITS OF GUIDING PRINCIPLES

Your core values support your vision, shape your culture, and reflect what your company stands for. They are the essence of the company's identity. Therefore, you can only define your company's guiding principles once you have a clear understanding of both your own vision and your company's.

Establishing strong guiding principles creates three main advantages for your company:

1. **Guiding principles support the decision-making process.** For example, if one of your guiding principles is to stand behind the quality of your products, any products not reaching satisfactory standards are automatically eliminated. You'd be surprised at how often your guiding principles can help you answer day-to-day questions.

2. **Guiding principles teach clients and potential customers what your company is about.** They also clarify the identity of your company. In our often-aggressive world, you create a competitive advantage whenever you successfully communicate what your company stands for.

3. **Guiding principles are important recruiting and retention tools.** Today's job seekers do their homework. They know a lot about the companies they apply to, and research consistently shows working for a company that shares their own values is tremendously important to them.

In other words, while your guiding principles may sound abstract, they can lead to some very real benefits.

HOW DO YOU FIND YOUR GUIDING PRINCIPLES?

Core values are not one-size-fits-all. In his article, "Aligning Action and Values," business writer Jim Collins says organizational values can't be set. You must discover them. Unfortunately, too many companies mistakenly pick their core values out of thin air and try to fit them to their organization.

Here are two tips to determine the guiding principles that are right for you:

1. **Get your team.** This could be just you, or it could include any other partners, founders, or team members who were around in the early stages of your company. In fact, it could include anyone who just seems to get it. If you regularly talk business with your significant other, for instance, then they will likely have some good insights for you.

2. **Ask your team: What are our organization's core values or guiding principles?** You may need to facilitate some discussion around this topic first to get the ideas rolling. Guiding principles should be a short sentence rather than a single word, like a sound bite. You'll find it's much easier to brainstorm that way.

Here are some examples of strong guiding principles:

- Embrace and drive change.
- Create fun and a little weirdness.
- Anticipate, embrace, and thrive on change.
- Be adventurous, creative, and open-minded.
- Run it like we own it.
- Pursue growth and learning.
- Build open and honest relationships with communication.
- Build a positive team and family spirit under the spirit of friendly competition.
- Do more with less.
- Work hard and have fun as a team.
- Be passionate and determined.
- Be humble.
- Everything should be passionate, profitable, and done with fun.

Get the idea? Now you try.

VALUES CHECK

With your core principles in place, ask yourself and your team the following three questions:

1. Will these guiding principles be as valid a hundred years from now as they are today?

2. Would you want your organization to hold to these guiding principles if they became a competitive disadvantage?

3. If you started a new organization in a different industry tomorrow, would you use these same guiding principles?

If your sound bites can endure these three questions, then you've got yourself a guiding principle. Now compile them, publish them for everyone in your company, and encourage everyone to use them in their decision-making processes. Don't worry, there's no such thing as using these principles too much.

As Mohandas Gandhi said, "Your beliefs become your thoughts, your thoughts become your words, your words become your habits, your habits become your values, and your values become your destiny." The more you and your team members keep your guiding principles in mind, the more your organization will reflect them through direct action.

CRITICAL SUCCESS FACTORS

Now that we've covered vision and values, you're probably ready to get going on your business objectives and goals.

I understand. After all, when you meet your objectives and goals, you make your money. However, first, we need to talk about your critical success factors.

A company's critical success factors bring its vision to life. They are your foundation, the base holding the rest of your business plan in place.

For some business owners, their critical success factors are immediately apparent. Often, they revolve around sales, managing their team, and building strong processes.

To help you determine your own critical success factors, here are nine fundamental questions.

#1: WHAT PRODUCT OR SERVICE REQUIRES DEVELOPMENT?

Do you need to compete more effectively with a new product? Is another company taking market share away from you because you don't have a product or service that competes with it? If the answer is yes, then it's time to get developing. It may be critical to your success.

#2: WHAT PROCESSES NEED DEVELOPMENT?

More importantly, do you have the *right* processes in place—and are they being used? Think about this. If you hired a new junior team member, would their role, their responsibilities, and your expectations of them be readily available for them to read, learn, and adopt?

#3: DOES EXCELLENCE, COST, OR CLIENT IMPACT NEED TO BE PRIORITIZED IN YOUR COMPANY?

Here's an example of what I mean. Many business owners say customer loyalty is important to them, but how strong is it already? If you're stable here while another area is lacking, it may be time to shift priorities.

#4: WHAT MARKET AREAS NEED TO BE EXPANDED UPON?

If you keep seeing opportunities with customers outside your core geography, do you need to reevaluate where your geography is? Do you need to develop more web-based solutions? Do you need to open another office? Conversely, if you have an office that is not performing well, do you need to contract your locations?

#5: HOW CAN YOU BOOST CAPACITY OR EFFICIENCY?

Is there something you can do to reduce overhead or per-unit cost? You may need to excel at increasing outputs, but there may be more cost-effective ways of delivering products or services.

#6: WHAT IMPROVED TECHNOLOGY OR KNOW-HOW IS NEEDED?

Sometimes our companies need to go out and find the right technology to help us become more efficient. Sometimes we can investigate new technology that we've heard of and evaluate whether it will make us more efficient.

#7: WHAT IMPROVEMENTS ARE NEEDED IN YOUR MARKETING—STRATEGY, TACTICS, MEASUREMENT, OR PEOPLE?

Do you understand who your target buyers are and what kinds of marketing materials they would find most compelling? Do you need to work with an agency to help with your branding? Do you have an established presence online and on social media channels? What about automated systems for identifying and following up with leads?

#8: WHAT IMPROVEMENTS TO YOUR DISTRIBUTION METHOD OR ORDERING SYSTEMS ARE NEEDED?

You could have the greatest product or service in the world, but if you can't reliably get them to your customers, then it won't matter.

#9: DO YOU NEED TO CHANGE THE LOCATION OF YOUR HEADQUARTERS OR DISTRIBUTION PLANTS?

This may help you become more competitive. Is your business exactly where you want it to be?

OBJECTIVES AND GOALS

Now, it's time for the fun part.

The best objectives and goals satisfy your critical success factors. The following are some guiding principles to help you. For each, take some time to write four or five objective goals for your business.

BE SMART

This is business 101, but it bears repeating: Set smart goals. Create objectives that are specific, measurable, achievable, realistic, and time-bound. Anything that can be measured *should* be measured regularly. This is how you turn your subjective vision and values into a clear, objective process.

WRITE EVERYTHING DOWN

Once you know your goals, don't forget to write them down. Here are examples:

- Sell my business for $2 million before the end of the year.
- Restructure the marketing department with one fewer team member headcount and a lower operating cost.
- Launch new product X with a market penetration of 20 percent of our existing customer base within a four-month period.

See? Setting goals doesn't have to be an overwrought process. While they depend on sound thinking, the simpler and more actionable your goals are, the better.

EXECUTE THE PLAN

With your goals in place, it's time to decide a few other things:

- Who's in charge?

- What are the deadlines?
- How can you measure progress?

For each goal, decide what strategies you need to achieve it. Each strategy will then need an accompanying set of tactics to support it, and this is exactly what we're going to cover in the rest of the book.

KEEPING YOUR BUSINESS STATEMENT RELEVANT

Congratulations! Whether you've realized it or not, you've just written your very own business plan. With that out of the way, here's the million-dollar question: Why is your business plan going to be more successful than the 1 percent of people who keep theirs locked away and forgotten?

Two reasons:

1. Your business plan can fit on one piece of paper.
2. That piece of paper will hold not only your personal and business vision statements, but also your critical success factors, goals, and strategies.

With your *why* on one side and your *how* on the other, that document will be a lot more valuable, won't it?

Finally, here's my last suggestion. It's something I've seen many business owners take to heart. Tape your sheet of paper to the side of your computer screen or pin it to a nearby board or wall. That way, you can remind yourself what you're trying to achieve every single day.

Keep your goals and strategies facing outward, as you may not want to share your personal vision with everyone who comes to your office. Even if you can't see your vision statement, however, you'll know it's there. *You'll know why you're in business.*

NOW FOR SOME FUN

There are some really great values that business owners have. What are the most fun, your business or those you've heard of?

Once you've given it some thought, share here:

http://exactlywhereyouwanttobe.com/what

PART II

THE TEN ROADS

Congratulations! You made it through Part I.

Now we get into it.

You're about to find killer strategies and cool tactics that will take your business to the next level in the following areas:

- Leadership—getting yourself and others exactly where you want to be
- Marketing (hint: it's all about your story)
- Sales, the most feared word in all of business
- More sales, but this time, with a team
- Sticking to what you love and outsourcing the rest
- Bringing on team members

- Bringing passion, profitability, and happiness to your team
- Operations (no, not the board game)
- Fine-tuning your dream
- Thinking long-term and planning ahead

There is a logical order to these chapters. However, let's not get too tied up with convention (we *are* entrepreneurs, after all). If you see a chapter that's more important or urgent to you and your needs than another, head there now.

It's okay. We're not judging.

Let's all reconvene at the concluding chapter once you've taken your journey.

CHAPTER 4

PRODUCTIVITY IN LEADERSHIP

---

*Success consists of going from failure
to failure without lost enthusiasm.*

—WINSTON CHURCHILL

Meet George. When he was a child, George and his family emigrated from Croatia to the United States. An excellent student, George quickly leveraged his degree at UCLA into a successful engineering career, honing his skill set while working at a number of well-regarded companies.

In 1988, George had the track record and know-how to start his own company, PENCO Civil Engineering.[13] Beginning with one of its earliest projects, Disneyland's

---

13   http://www.pencoeng.com

Toontown, PENCO has left an unmistakable mark on Southern California and is now home to over thirty team members.

PENCO has succeeded in part because of George's commitment to crafting winning pitches and all-around high business standards. George is not only a great communicator, but he's also honest and passionate. When I first met him, I asked George why he loved engineering so much. His response was simple: his work touched people and made their lives better.

With such a dedicated leader at the helm, it was only a matter of time before others in the industry took notice. Sure enough, George quickly received multiple offers to purchase PENCO from rival firms—and by 2007, he was ready to sell. Unfortunately, before he could get his plans and evaluations in place, the Great Recession of 2008 scared away potential suitors, who were understandably more concerned with saving their own companies.

George remained steadfast. Even if it meant waiting, he was confident he could not only sell PENCO, but also get his asking price. In the meantime, PENCO forged ahead and continued to build on its past successes.

By 2016, George was ready to try again, so he hired a mergers and acquisitions (M&A) company to shepherd the process. When the firm failed to deliver enough serious suitors over the next year, George doubled down on PENCO's team, quality, and sales, as well as his leadership.

As of this writing, PENCO is doing extremely well, with an expanded and experienced team, exciting projects, and healthy financial projections. Because George persevered, he's now on the road to a comfortable retirement.

WHAT'S THE SECRET OF SUCCESS?

Perseverance.

Yes, whether in life or in business, it really is that simple. True leaders know how to gain momentum *and* how to maintain it. They keep going no matter what, adapting to changing circumstances as needed, and making sure to learn a little something about themselves along the way.

George's story may be a model of perseverance, but I'm willing to bet your own story shares some similarities. Take a moment to ask yourself the following questions:

- How is your own journey similar to George's?

- Did you move to another city, state, or country before setting out on your own, like so many other successful business leaders?
- Did you learn a trade from other businesses and mentors before setting out on your own?
- Do you have the same belief in yourself and passion for your industry?
- Are you willing to persevere like George has?

Regardless of how you answer these questions, remember: *You* choose to persevere. Remind yourself of this daily and let it motivate you.

THE FOUR FACTORS OF GREAT LEADERS

However big or small your business, no matter where you've been or where you're going, if you want to lead your company toward a brighter tomorrow, you must embrace the following four traits:

- Productivity
- Motivation
- Ability to Sell
- Awareness

The rest of this chapter will examine each of these factors in greater detail.

LEADERSHIP FACTOR #1: PRODUCTIVITY

Quantity over quality. The greatest leaders always seem to get more done. They power through work without skimping on quality and still manage to enjoy hobbies and family time.

It's easy to wonder how. Great leaders are a lot of things, but they're not time travelers. They face the same constraints as you or I.

However, they make the most of their available time. Maintaining and maximizing productivity is the key to staying organized, overcoming work-related stress, and meeting deadlines and commitments.

How do you manage it? Here are four productivity tips just for you.

#1: Master the Workweek

The more you come into each week with a plan for how you will spend your time, the more you will get done. For optimal productivity, consider breaking up your workweek in the following ways.

Work on *the Business, Not* in *It.*

No matter the size or profitability of your business, set aside at least five hours a week to focus on improving your processes, developing or refining systems, and honing or creating your vision.

You're right. This is not easy. Better to be earning money when a client or potential client or customer calls.

Stop. That's short-termism. Plan your future for fun and profit by dedicating this time every week.

Take Time for Yourself

Your business amplifies your strengths and weaknesses, making self-development crucial. Invest a minimum of five hours each week for personal development. This can encompass activities like exercising, reading, or working with a coach.

Yes, this is also hard. You know the saying, "They are working for the business?" Well, don't let that happen to you.

Set a Schedule

Scheduling is the easiest way to stay organized and on track. Allow two hours per week to get your to-do list out of your head and onto your calendar.

So many business owners are overworked and stressed out. Say "no" to that "right here, right now" feeling. Schedule your time.

Manage Expectations

Don't set unattainable goals. My to-do list used to have twenty items on it, and I rarely got them all done. I recommend focusing on just two or three objectives per day. Empower yourself by setting boundaries and protecting yourself from unobtainable goals. If you don't, you'll lose all of your passion quickly.

Leave Room

Interruptions happen. The unexpected occurs. Leave some buffer time in your daily schedule to deal with these things. Allow between three and five hours a week for the unexpected—or forty-five minutes to an hour each day.

Be aware that unexpected interruptions come from within just as frequently as they come from others. Ever caught yourself falling down a search engine rabbit hole or in a daze looking at social media?

It happens. You can't stop it. But, you can leave room for it.

If you don't need all that time, give yourself permission to leave work early. It may sound crazy when it feels like there's always something else you can be doing, but the occasional early dismissal will help keep you sane in the long run.

#2: Embrace the Impossible

Many business owners feel like they can never catch up. They're used to reacting to one urgent need after another and can never imagine breaking their week down in the way I just described. In fact, most of the leaders I coach worry they don't have enough time to work with me.

If this sounds like you, don't worry. I understand. That's why I made these chapters short.

That said, proper time management is essential to getting your business exactly where you want it to be. In fact, it's a key driver of success. Focus on adopting a system that makes sense to both your personal and business needs. Here are a few mantras to help you out.

Avoid Multitasking

Contrary to popular belief, multitasking doesn't save any time. It simply means you're not focused on the task at hand and aren't performing at your peak. Your brain may move rapidly from one task to another, but there's a cost to this kind of switching. In the end, you won't perform any of your many tasks as well as you could.

Want to manage your time better? Take this pledge:

I, _____, for the benefit of myself and my business, commit to never multitask.

Signed,

_____

Play to Your Strengths

You undoubtedly wear many hats within your organization, but you know your strengths. Identify the two or three roles in which you excel, focus on those, and delegate the rest.

Get Organized

Combine meeting schedules and to-do lists into a single, cohesive calendar and schedule your day in thirty-minute increments. Include every task, however small, that you need to complete.

Schedule to Reschedule

Pay attention to your scheduling, make note of what worked and what didn't, and adjust your approach the following week. Work on this skill constantly.

#3: Delegate

Yes, you are better at doing anything within your business than anyone else. However, being your company's Jack or Jill of all trades can seriously inhibit your freedom. Trust your team and delegate wherever you can.

This is the single most important factor if your business employs fewer than three people. If you continue to do everything yourself, you'll never get over this tactically, and it will become impossible to grow your business.

Delegating slows down your business initially. As you find tasks to delegate, you are going to have to train someone, ask them to write up a process for the future, and check their work. It's all very time-consuming.

Do not—I repeat—do *not* avoid this. It is the secret to long-term efficiency.

#4: Say No

The single most important word for a business owner is "*no*." Keep a to-*don't* list. Stay focused and get used to saying "no" to yourself and others.

Sorry, there are no hidden strategies for this one. The best way to say *no* is to say *no*.

LEADERSHIP FACTOR #2: MOTIVATION

Getting motivated and staying motivated is the key to long-term productivity. Anybody can muster the motivation to get started, but the most successful business leaders know how to keep pushing toward the finish line even when others have thrown in the towel.

What do you need to stay motivated? To quote the great philosophers of our time, "Tell me what you want, what you really, really want."

Believe me, The Spice Girls know what they're talking about. Wishing you were more motivated? Start with a clear idea of what you want, where you're going, and why you want to get there.[14]

Before we get into the following tips, let's go Goldilocks for a moment. One of the key factors to staying motivated is being challenged to the edge of your abilities. Trying something that is too easy will bore you. And trying something that is too hard will discourage you. You need challenges that are just right.

Breaking Down Your Goals

Having a clear vision of your goals is a great start. But what are goals anyway? In my experience, three essential elements make up every goal:

- **Talent:** The rate at which your skills improve with effort
- **Skill:** The byproduct of the time spent honing your craft
- **Achievement:** The application of skills toward a goal

These traits are often confused, but they are nevertheless distinct. Everyone comes preloaded with some degree of

---

14 This is such a crucial endeavor that the first part of this book is dedicated to this very concept. Did you make sure to read it? If you jumped in at this point, go back and read it.

talent, but talent is nothing more than unmet potential. Only effort can help you convert a talent into a skill.

Similarly, skill alone is not the same as achievement. Effort builds skill, but effort also makes skill productive. Without effort, your skill is nothing more than what you could have done but didn't. It's up to you to apply your skills if you hope to achieve your goals.

By recognizing these stages, we begin to see that motivation isn't an abstract concept, but a process that any of us can apply.

Embracing Grit

Another part of motivation is what many refer to as good, old-fashioned grit. In the simplest terms, grit is simply perseverance and passion for your long-term goals. Grit may sound like an innate trait that you either have or don't, but the reality is that grit can be developed and harnessed.

According to business leader Angela Duckworth, who has written and spoken extensively on the concept, there are four elements of grit:

1. **Interest.** Passion begins with intrinsically enjoying what you do. Remember that interests must be trig-

gered again and again (and again). Find ways to make that happen—and have patience. Developing your interests takes time.

2. **Practice.** One form of perseverance is the daily discipline of trying to do things better than the day before.

3. **Purpose.** Passion comes easy with the conviction that your work matters.

4. **Hope.** Forget the glass is half-empty or half-full debate. Instead, think of hope as a kind of perseverance, an ability to rise to the occasion.

Are you ready to get gritty? Set a purposeful goal and keep heading toward it one step at a time. The only way to overcome challenges and get up when you fall down is through daily investment in your goals.[15]

LEADERSHIP FACTOR #3: ABILITY TO SELL

Regardless of your industry, if you're a business owner, you sell—not just to clients, but to everyone. You sell to your team, to your stakeholders, to your partners, to your vendors, to the agencies you hire, and to your banker.

---

15 To learn more about Angela Duckworth's work with the concept of grit, I recommend her book *Grit: The Power of Passion and Perseverance* (Collins, 2016), her TED Talk, or one of her many research papers.

Sales may have nothing to do with your official title or your key skills, but that doesn't matter. You are a salesperson nevertheless.

Once you've accepted this fact, there's only one thing to do: sell well and try to prosper—but don't sell to your loved ones if you value an authentic lifestyle.[16]

We've got lots to discuss on the subject of sales. See Chapters 6 and 7 for strategies on selling on your own and selling with a team, respectively.

LEADERSHIP FACTOR #4: AWARENESS

Despite the claims of traditional business books, a true mark of a great leader is their awareness of themselves, others, and their surroundings:

- **Self-awareness** is essential for recognizing and understanding your mental and emotional health, your mental agility, and your physical capabilities.
- **Awareness of others** refers to anyone you're working with, from your customers to your team. Take the time to understand their wants and needs, why they behave

---

16 This goes right back to the work/life integration we discussed in Chapter 1. This is a crucial concept, so, if you haven't already, go back and read this book from the beginning. Don't say I didn't warn you.

in a particular way, and how they feel. The deeper your understanding, the better your business can be.

- **Awareness of your surroundings.** The space around you is positively brimming with valuable tidbits that can save you both time and effort. Science shows that while the human brain receives 11 million bits of information per second, it consciously only absorbs about fifty.

Half of the journey of becoming more aware is simply recognizing your need to do it. So, on that note, congratulations! You're already halfway there.

To get the rest of the way there, I recommend the following nine daily tactics.

#1: Write Your Way

When you clearly write your strategy out, you're 50 percent more likely to succeed. If you share your goals with someone else, your chances of success increase to 75 percent.[17]

Try this:

1. Write down a single goal you'd like to accomplish for the day.

---

17 We covered this in detail in Part I. This is your final warning to catch up!

2. Think of a few ways in which you could sabotage your efforts to reach your goal.

3. Write out counter-strategies to overcome your own self-sabotage.

Following these steps will give you a clear picture of where you're going, what could obstruct you, and how to overcome it. If a fifteen-second exercise like this can help you in a day, imagine what could be achieved if you spent a few minutes on this. Instead of looking at what you want to accomplish just for today, you could look ahead to the next week, month, and year.

#2: Yawn

Stretch slowly. Gently stroke your hands and arms. Try it—it works. This is not a book on physiology, so let's not waste time on the explanation. Just believe, and we can move on.

#3: Use a Mindfulness Alarm

Do you want to lower your stress levels and increase your productivity? Download an awareness clock app. Set an hourly (or random) reminder to take a one-minute mental break to relax and be aware of yourself and those around you.[18]

---

18 Disclaimer: If you have a job that could result in danger to yourself or others if you were to take this mindfulness time, I advise you to skip this one.

#4: Live Your Values

Every day, ask yourself, "What is my most important value?" If you've filled out your one-page strategic plan from Part I, you already know the answer. Now, it's up to you to live by your values.

#5: Take Pleasure Breaks

Take one minute every hour to do something pleasurable. Stretch, do sixty seconds of aerobics, wash your face—anything you enjoy. Doing this releases dopamine that stimulates the motivational center of your brain, pushing you to work harder and more efficiently.

#6: Trust Your Intuition

You know that small voice in your head that tells you when something or someone isn't right, even when the evidence tells you otherwise? Trust it. If something doesn't feel right, it isn't.

#7: List Your Accomplishments

Listing your daily accomplishments increases your awareness of what makes you successful. Better still, play *show and tell* with friends or family over a drink or a meal. If you have a family with kids and you're home, this is one of the most fun exercises you can do daily while taking turns with the whole family.

#8: Use Fewer Words

Humans can only focus on roughly ten words in ten seconds. Hammer home your critical points by staying within this limit. Adopting a minimalist approach raises your awareness of both your own communication and that of others.

#9: Sleep Better, Think Better

If you, like many other business leaders, wake up and have trouble getting back to sleep, find three words that make you feel secure and relaxed and that resonate with you deeply—for example, *peace*, *love*, and *god*.

If you're still having trouble getting back to sleep, write down the anxieties keeping you awake. This reassures your brain you'll take care of the issues in the morning. Then, repeat your three words—your mantra—over and over, shutting out all other thoughts until sleep finds you. The better you sleep, the better you think, and the more aware you become.

DO YOU WANT TO BE BRILLIANT?

Want to know a little extra secret to success? Consider this:

Brilliant people exhibit true genius infrequently and in small bursts.

This might sound preposterous, but it's true. Einstein published 248 papers in his lifetime, but his most important works came early on. Mozart, Bach, and Beethoven were prolific composers, but only a handful of their pieces are considered masterpieces.

In other words, there's no need to burden yourself with the expectation of daily brilliance. Even Einstein and Mozart didn't live up to that standard. Why should you? If you put in the work, focus on mindfulness, and keep developing your skills, you'll find no shortage of great—and occasionally brilliant—business success.

MY FIRST BUSINESS

When I was a child, I enjoyed school and knew I was clever, but I didn't excel and couldn't get the grades I wanted. By nine, I learned I had dyslexia, which was a far less common diagnosis in the early 1980s than it is today. Since the British government paid for dyslexic kids to attend boarding school, by the age of ten, I found myself in a strange new environment far from home.

Apart from the lack of moving staircases and living paintings, my boarding school looked and felt exactly like Hogwarts. I learned quickly that everyone had to find their own niche, something I struggled to do for much of my first year. I wasn't especially athletic, and although I had a core group of friends, I certainly wasn't the popular kid.

By eleven, however, I discovered an entrepreneurial talent of which I had previously been unaware. It began with the realization that, especially for a young boy, boarding school is restrictive. Everything is structured and organized, and there isn't a great deal of free time or freedom. Most of the time, my movement was limited to the school grounds.

In this environment, I surmised I could make a handy profit selling *Playboy* magazines to my fellow students. After all, demand was high and supply was nonexistent. While I couldn't walk to the store and buy a copy, I could have them mailed to me. So I did, selling them at a markup to my friends.

Eventually, it occurred to me that my business model was wrong. Eleven-year-old boys don't have much cash, so I couldn't mark the magazines up too much. Further, I was only making a one-time profit and simultaneously creating a secondhand market. Neither was good for business.

The budding entrepreneur in me persevered. Eventually, I came up with a solution by creating a *Playboy* library and renting the magazines out for a smaller fee. This way, I retained ownership of all the assets, eradicated the secondhand market, and made a better profit.

THE PASSION, PROFITABILITY, AND HAPPINESS INDEX

Even with my first business, I learned the value of the three key traits of successful leadership:

- **Passion:** I had a great passion for this work. As funny as it might sound looking back, my little *Playboy* library was my identity at the time.
- **Profit:** In a very closed business market environment and relative to the earning potential of an eleven-year-old boy, this venture was highly profitable.
- **Happiness:** It probably goes without saying, but these products made my pubescent friends very happy. In turn, this helped increase my social standing at the school, a win-win-win situation for me, my classmates, and my first business.

The moral of the story? Find what you're good at, own it, and adapt as you go. In this case, I made kids happy, I made my friends happy, and I made money at the same time.

FINAL TAKEAWAYS

You're now well on your way to realizing your vision, freeing yourself from your business, and finding a balance between passion, profit, and happiness. You know how to maximize your productivity, drive motivation, and increase your awareness.

When considering productivity in leadership, here are the three most important takeaways:

1. You need to be a great leader to create a successful business.
2. To be a great leader, you need productivity, motivation, sales skill, and awareness.
3. Trust your intuition.

That's it. Now you have everything you need to go forth and be brilliant. But don't go just yet. We've got plenty of unmissable stuff coming in the next chapters.

NOW FOR SOME FUN

Just like with every chapter in this book, now it's time to share your wisdom with other business owners.

Here, the question is: What motivates you?

Once you've given it some thought, share here:

http://exactlywhereyouwanttobe.com/productivity

CHAPTER 5

MARKETING YOUR STORY

———

Marketing is no longer about the stuff that you make, but about the stories you tell.

—SETH GODIN

Meet Melissa. She epitomizes the four factors of a great leader—productivity, motivation, sales, and awareness. Melissa started in printing, but when that industry began to struggle, she and her business partner adapted. Bolstered by Melissa's keen business acumen and design skills, she launched TC Two, a highly successful boutique design and marketing company.[19]

---

19 www.tctwo.com

As soon as we began working together, I could see that sales weren't an issue for Melissa. In fact, she closed with over half the prospects she sat down with—a far higher rate than the industry average.

Like many other business leaders with exceptional sales, Melissa considered marketing her primary challenge. She may have put ads out here and there, but she didn't have an integrated marketing plan in place to optimize her efforts.

To address this, we worked on creating a measured, structured plan that successfully incorporated multiple simultaneous elements. Her marketing plan was now more ambitious, but more importantly, it was also more flexible, which allowed her to adapt as the market shifted around her.

Since she put this marketing plan in place, her business has seen a 20 percent revenue increase each year. With more leads and prospects coming down the pipeline, Melissa can focus on what she does best—closing deals and working with customers she has the most fun with.

WHAT *IS* MARKETING?

Seth Godin defines marketing as visibility and credibility—in other words, making people aware of you and convincing them you're the best option.

Every business wants their target audience to know they offer products or services that prospective customers want or need. My coaching business is a prime example. Before I wrote this book, I had a database of 2,000 potential customers. Since publication, my visibility, database, and sales have increased significantly.

Once they're aware of you, your prospects need to know you can deliver. The prospects I meet with, for instance, often ask up-front why my services are their best option. While I usually describe past success and triumphs, admittedly any other business coach can do the same thing.

Finally, I settled on another point of difference: a published book on business coaching, which gives me more credibility—and which you're now reading.

CAN YOU ANSWER WHY?

Let's look at a little messaging magic that Simon Sinek brought to the world. Your customers need to know your *why*. Why should they buy from you? Why your product or service?

Melissa at TC Two originally answered her *why* with a traditional feature/benefit-style business statement:

> TC Two is a leading branding and marketing company providing online and traditional services to help businesses reach new customers and increase sales.

Not bad, but look what happens when we alter the order of sentiment to why, how, what:

> At TC2, we help businesses increase sales through the implementation of online and traditional design and promotional services because we're a leading branding and marketing company.

The words and the basic message are still the same, but the restructuring gives the reader a cause early on, resulting in a more favorable reception.

Take a few minutes and try the same for your company. Write out your succinct company message using the why, how, what format. Once you're happy with the message, have your team update your website and marketing collateral to include it. It may seem like a small thing, but honing your company's message goes a long way in increasing sales.

IDEAL CUSTOMERS

Who exactly are your ideal customers, and are you targeting the right ones? Who will help you achieve your vision and get you where you want to be?

If you're not sure, it's time to create a customer persona—or possibly multiple personas.

Give your ideal customer a name. Then fill out key demographics:

- Age
- Gender
- Income
- Geography

Be sure to include any characteristics, goals, and objectives that define this persona. Key attributes for my core group of customers include:

- Businesses generating more than $1 million in annual revenue
- Been in business for at least three years

- Have three or more team members
- Aged forty-plus
- Reside in any English-speaking country

Once you've established your core customer demographics, consider their psychographics. This includes their outlook, opinions, interests, attitudes, and values. For my coaching business, my core customer psychographics look something like this:

- Optimistic outlook
- Value family time
- Enjoy domestic and international travel
- Thrive on challenges
- Love their job
- Homeschool their children
- Enjoy champagne

Now you have your ideal customer persona—the people with whom you want to do the most business. Members of this group will help you maximize profit and minimize effort. They will help you achieve your goals and get you where you want to be.

Build your marketing efforts, as well as every other facet of your business, around your ideal customer persona. Every touchpoint, including sales, customer service, and delivery, should reflect the personalities and needs of your target audience.

WHERE CAN YOU FIND THEM?

Not that you've identified your target customer personas, it's time to establish where they gather. Do they like movies, tradeshows, sporting events, or the local wine shop? Do they spend time on specific websites? Where do they shop? Are they in one geographic region?

Once you've answered those questions, explore the advertising and sponsorship opportunities available. If, for example, these prospects most commonly frequent a specific grocery store, you could advertise on a billboard right outside the store or place smaller ads on the shopping carts.

Alternatively, find out where your target audience spends time online. Promote ads on these sites, or create some high-quality blog content that showcases your expertise.

WHO CAN YOU PARTNER WITH?

If you want to mitigate the risk of investing large sums in new marketing opportunities, or if your budget simply isn't that big, consider partnering up. Find a business that doesn't directly compete but does complement your services. Build a good relationship, promote each other's business, refer prospects, and engage in joint marketing activities.

When choosing a partner company, the most important element to consider is the person you'll be working with. If you see eye-to-eye and have a history together, your relationship has the right foundation to build upon. It *can't* be forced, so please don't try.

Ramping it up a notch, if you find a *really* good partner, you'll be blown away by the speed and brute force power your marketing will have.

SCREEN YOUR CUSTOMERS

Now that you know exactly who your primary customers are, work to limit the time and resources you expend on secondary and tertiary prospects. While most business owners are happy to close any sale that comes their way, when those sales involve anyone other than your primary customer profile, it actually detracts from your long-term business goals.

Here's your chance to toughen up. Make a stand and only engage with prospects who fall into your ideal or primary profile. Prospects don't have to check off every box, but if they meet the majority of your criteria, you should consider them an ideal or primary customer.

Ultimately, this involves weeding out the secondary and tertiary prospects before they become customers. Give your team a set of screening questions, perhaps in the form of an online quiz, and add the scores to your customer relationship management (CRM) system.

HOW ARE YOU GETTING YOUR SALES?

Just like with my client Melissa at TC2, marketing is rarely a business owner's primary skill. Referrals and word-of-mouth sales may sustain them in the short term, but it's important to create other viable avenues for growth and sustainability.

HOW MUCH DO YOU SPEND ON MARKETING?

Most small- to medium-sized businesses devote only a small budget to marketing. This often results in lower-than-ideal sales figures. To succeed with your business, it's important that you learn to strike a balance between your sales and marketing budgets—and to unify everything with a comprehensive marketing strategy.

HOW MUCH SHOULD YOU SPEND ON MARKETING?

Instead of asking how much you should spend on marketing, try a different question: What's your return on investment (ROI) for your marketing spend? The truth is, it doesn't really matter how much you're spending if you are making a solid return on your investment.

When factoring cost, remember:

- Include every tiny expense, not just the actual ad or campaign cost.
- In the real world, returns aren't guaranteed, but you *can* determine the probability of achieving your desired return.
- Because you don't have an unlimited budget, determine which of the many potential places to spend your marketing dollars will net you the best return.

That's it! While more detail might go into each individual step, try not to make your overall spending strategy any more complicated than the process previously outlined. After all, keeping clear objectives often means keeping a simple process.

TRENDINESS WILL ONLY GET YOU SO FAR

Here's one bit of advice I share with many of my clients: blindly following the latest marketing trends is no better than sticking to the obsolete marketing practices of the past.

For instance, social media certainly has its place, but it's not effective as a stand-alone marketing effort. In fact, in all the companies I've worked with, I've only ever seen one significant sale come directly from a platform like Twitter—and at the time, it wasn't being used as a stand-alone marketing strategy.

Who do I know that had that bit of Twitter success? It just so happens to be Melissa's company, TC Two. Go ahead, ask her how she bagged Tesla as a customer for one of her engineering clients. It's a great story.

Here's the bottom line: No single marketing action, whether it's Twitter or something else—will bring you your desired return on marketing spend. Unfortunately, many small businesses still fall into the trendiness trap.

EVERY CENT COUNTS, SO COUNT EVERY CENT

When establishing your marketing strategy and planning your marketing actions, count every cent, including the cost of your time. This precise balancing requires you to focus on the importance of combined measurement. Let's look at a couple examples to clarify.

#1: BUDGET OVER TIME

Say you've decided to take out a one-page ad in *The New York Times*, with its impressive daily readership of 626,000 people. The ad itself costs about $150,000, but don't forget the cost of ad design, page placement, and your own time investment orchestrating the ad, which could be under four hours. Here, the time investment is minimal, but the cost is high.

#2: TIME OVER BUDGET

In this situation, you decide to join the group, Business Network International (BNI). Yearly membership dues are $500. That's a relatively low financial outlay, but what about the time commitment? When you join BNI, you commit to attending weekly seventy-five-minute meetings, not to mention the prep time, other one-on-one meetings, training, communication, and so on. In all, a membership with BNI comes with a low financial cost, but a commitment to over eighty hours of your time a year.

CHOOSING THE BEST APPROACH

What's the right approach for you? I can answer that.

Look back at your personal and business vision. Then look at your financial accounts. If sales growth is critical to your business, but you need to spend less time at work, then example 1 will work for you. If, by contrast, you love networking and want to be active in your community, then example 2 is the way to go. Just possibly, you'll need a mixture of both.

DESIGNING YOUR MARKETING STRATEGY

Now that we've covered some of the basics—what marketing is, how much you should expect to spend, and avoiding trends without a larger goal—let's start designing a marketing strategy that works for you.

THE BASICS

If you haven't noticed by now, I'm a big fan of covering the basics. They're the earmark of any good business strategy, but are all too often ignored. Start with the following questions when designing your marketing strategy:

- **Who?** Your ideal customers. Your customer persona tells you who they are. Put that at the top of your plan, just like I put them at the beginning of this chapter.
- **Why?** What are the reasons your primary audience should or would want to buy from you? Yes, we covered that after customer personas.
- **Where?** Refer to the ideal consumer profile and identify where your primary customer lives.
- **What?** What's the next step you want your primary prospects to take? We'll discuss this more later, but for now, just know that your marketing must guide the prospect through the journey from awareness to purchase.
- **How?** How are you going to reach your primary customers? Refine the ideas and tactics you began compiling earlier in this chapter, such as social media, advertising, networking, media relations, events and tradeshows, brochures, leaflets, business directories, direct mail, email, video, speaking engagements, point of sale, displays, product placement, referrals, SEO, sponsorships, and surveys/research. List these possible tactics (and you may have multiple ideas for each tactic), and alongside each one, record the following information:
  - Dedicated time, date, or duration
  - Preferred partner
  - Total cost

- Total time cost
- Revenue potential
- Probability of achieving that revenue potential
- Anticipated return on investment (ROI)

Use this list to establish which tactics to prioritize or eliminate. Remember that you need to run these campaigns throughout the year. After all, you don't want to use up your marketing budget too quickly or overwhelm your sales or delivery resources.

THE ACTION PLAN

With your tactics in place, use a spreadsheet (or equivalent) to create an action plan with the following categories:

- Name of tactic
- Date, time, duration
- Who is ultimately responsible for executing the plan
- Start date
- Top-level actions required for successful execution
- Who is responsible for each action
- Required budget
- Anticipated ROI
- Actual ROI

Keep each plan under one page and update the plan in real time to ensure it is an accurate snapshot.

MEASURING AND MAXIMIZING THROUGH IMC

It's crucial that you gauge the effectiveness of every campaign. To optimize your marketing plan, establish an integrated marketing communications (IMC) strategy in which you run multiple marketing tactics all at once.

You may be wondering if IMC is right for you. I say absolutely! In fact, I would argue it's right for anyone. Here are five reasons why:

1. **Cost-effectiveness.** Integrated marketing actually reduces your time cost by coordinating your marketing efforts.
2. **Media fragmentation.** The presence of so many different kinds of media means you need to diversify and integrate.
3. **Prospect sophistication.** Prospects are more easily motivated with messages from multiple mediums.
4. **Desire for interaction.** Prospects want to interact with you, not just be sold to, and that's easier with multiple lines of communication.
5. **Technology.** Marketing automation helps IMC campaigns run as smoothly as single-channel approaches.

As you can see, there are plenty of reasons to get started—and we haven't even covered the benefits yet. Here are my top five:

1. **Branding consistency.** Integrating all communications and marketing channels using identical branding and a consistent voice has greater impact.
2. **Consistent message.** The same message becomes more effective when used consistently across all marketing tools and platforms.
3. **Operational efficiency.** Integrated campaigns make better, more efficient use of creative resources.
4. **Cost-effectiveness.** Integrated communications cost less.
5. **Holistic reporting.** Individual reports are important to establish what resonates with your prospects and what doesn't, but IMC reporting across multiple channels and simultaneous campaigns gives you a more comprehensive dataset. You can use these results to refine and improve upon new campaigns.

One last thing on IMC. To make everything work, you need a clearly defined marketing plan and someone skilled at tactical coordination. Diving in without a plan is rarely a good idea.

STORYTELLING

Here's an old American Indian proverb that I've always loved: "Tell me a fact, and I'll learn. Tell me the truth, and I'll believe. Tell me a story, and it will live in my heart forever."

Storytelling is the key to every marketing campaign. It builds credibility, invokes emotional response, builds curiosity, and influences group thinking. Getting your storytelling elements right will make your marketing message feel effortless. Here are a few storytelling tips:

1. Know your audience.
2. Keep it simple.
3. Stay fresh.
4. Be honest.
5. Demonstrate credibility.
6. Spark interest.

You don't need a degree in literature to compose a compelling story. The basic formula consists of just eight elements:

- **The protagonist:** The hero
- **The antagonist:** The villain

- **The inciting incident:** The moment that drives the hero to action
- **The call to action:** The hero's goal
- **The dreadful alternative:** What happens if the hero fails
- **The conflict:** The progression of the quest or the fight, which drives the story
- **The supporting cast:** Those surrounding the hero and villain
- **The transformation:** The culmination of the hero's journey of growth

The conclusion is where most marketers struggle, so here are a few tried and tested endings:

- **And they lived happily ever after:** The conflict is resolved, the hero gets the object of their desire, and there's peace in the kingdom.
- **The moral of the story:** Conclude with a clear lesson.
- **The cliffhanger:** The story ends abruptly, leaving the audience guessing.
- **The universal truth:** Good defeats evil, or wisdom triumphs over ignorance.
- **Transformation:** A discovery changes the fate of the kingdom.

During my time in the film industry (more about that later), I learned there are two types of movies: extraordinary people in ordinary situations, or ordinary people in extraordinary situations. Either one makes a great foundation for your marketing story, but if you can think up a third option, more power to you.

PRICING

We're almost done with this chapter, but before we go, I want to give you a little more value and speak to one of my favorite marketing strategies.

ONLY FOUR PRICE-SETTING APPROACHES MATTER

Many business owners struggle with pricing—what to charge, whether they're being competitive, etc. While there's lots of conflicting advice, data, and analytics you could examine to set your prices, at the end of the day, it all comes down to choosing one of the following four top-level approaches.

#1: Cost-Based Pricing

Work out all of your overheads (O), including rent and utilities. Account for the cost of the materials (M) required to build your product. Figure out labor (L) costs, including your own time. Deduct those costs from the sale price (S), and you've got your profit (P):

$$S - (O + M + L) = P$$

#2: Quality-Based Pricing

Determine the quality of your offerings compared to the competition. If your products or services are superior, charge more. How much more depends on the items in question and how far superior your offerings are.

#3: Targeted Pricing

Specializing to focus solely on your ideal customers usually lets you charge a premium. A general accountant, for example, may charge $50 per hour. If they specialize in accountancy for veterinarians, however, they could charge $80 per hour.

#4: New Offerings Pricing

If you're launching a new product or service, a great way to establish price is to ask your ideal customers what they're willing to pay. Look at whether you can afford to sell at a reduced cost as a launch offer to get your product out there. How about a discount in exchange for a review or testimonial? Incentivize early adopters to refer others and help you achieve long-term success.

I ask my clients to go through this process and come back to me with their results. I then work out how to double the price—or even increase it by a factor of ten. Price is subjective, after all. You can charge anything as long as you can offer a good justification.

OTHER FACTORS AFFECTING PRICING

Sometimes, internal or external factors can also influence what you should charge. These include:

- **Inflation.** In the US, inflation increases, on average, by 3 percent annually. Increase your prices by the same amount every year to accommodate that increase.
- **Labor.** Monitor your labor cost, as a change here can radically affect profitability. Higher labor costs mean lower profit per sale unless you adjust prices accordingly.
- **Competition.** Competitive pricing is effective, but avoid a price war. Consider offering extra value rather than lowering prices.
- **Demand.** As demand for your product or service noticeably increases, it's time you increase your prices.

At the end of the day, don't be afraid to experiment. There are no guarantees regarding how a price change will impact sales. Just remember: lower isn't always better. In fact, if you lower your prices too much, you'll devalue your offerings, and prospects will assume your standards are also lower.

THE SECRET SAUCE: RAISING PRICES

When you take on a new customer, there are multiple acquisition costs. However, when you raise your prices across your existing customers, it's pure profit.

Let's throw some math at this to demonstrate. If a business has 1,000 customers who each spend $1,000 per year, that's $1,000,000 in revenue. Let's say the cost of goods is 50 percent ($500,000), and the overhead is 40 percent ($400,000). That leaves an annual profit of $100,000, without a price increase. To double its annual profit in this scenario, the business would need to double its customer base.

But look at what happens when the company raises its prices by just 20 percent. Spend per customer goes up to $1,200, putting the company's revenue up to $1,200,000. The cost of goods—$500,000—and the overhead—$400,000—remain the same. That leaves a profit of $300,000. That's a 300 percent increase in profit with the same number of customers for a 20 percent price increase.

Yes, it's true you could lose a few customers in this scenario. But that's not necessarily a bad thing. If this business raised its prices by 20 percent and lost 10 percent of its existing customers as a result, its annual profit would still increase substantially. With 900 customers spending $1,200 a year, your business would still net $1,080,000. Subtract the $500,000 cost of goods and the $400,000 overhead once again, and that's a profit of $140,000—a 40 percent increase in profitability with 10 percent fewer customers and 10 percent less work.

With the reduction in your workload comes other bonuses. You can spend more to acquire new customers, serve your customers better, and offer a better quality guarantee!

I know it can be scary to raise prices, but it is truly the easiest way to grow your profits. And at the end of the day, more profits mean more doors open for your business.

OTHER WAYS TO MAKE MORE MONEY

While the fastest way to make more money is to raise prices, here are other strategies you can try:

- Package or group goods at a discount.
- Offer a free prize (think of the makeup counter at Macy's).
- Offer a loyalty program to repeat customers.
- Up-sell (think of the famous "Would you like to Super-Size that?" up-sell at McDonald's).
- Create a premium version of your product and price it accordingly. Some customers always desire and demand the most expensive option available. It's who they are, so you might as well help them out.

Whatever approach you choose, make sure it aligns with your business. Remember, no one knows your business as well as you do. Get creative, try out new approaches, and have fun!

HOW I LEARNED THE VALUE OF STORYTELLING

After graduating boarding school, I went to college, where I studied psychology, delving into human nature and how we process stories. During my studies, I examined the ways stories are used to sell ideas, which propelled me into my career in marketing.

One story from my coursework has always stuck with me. In 1982, there was a ten-week conflict between Argentina and the United Kingdom that came to be known as the Falklands War. The Falkland Islands sit off the coast of Argentina, but at the time, they were British territories. In 1982, Argentina landed troops on the islands and declared their intention to reclaim sovereignty of the area.

Enter Margaret Thatcher, the British prime minister at the time, and a master storyteller. She understood not only how to tell a story, but also how to time it. For instance, Thatcher knew the most prominent TV news programs aired daily at 6:00 p.m. If she had a story she wanted to make public, she would inform news outlets at midday, giving them time to fact-check and prepare their coverage for the evening news. However, in instances where she didn't want a story covered, Mrs. Thatcher would delay speaking to reporters until 5:00 p.m., giving them very little time to prepare polished, factually accurate stories.

In the case of the Falklands War, Mrs. Thatcher went straight to the press and announced to the public that they had been caught complacent and unaware. She freely admitted that Britain had made a mistake, and then she proceeded to garner public support by tapping into British patriotism, national pride, and the legendary British stubborn streak. Her message was simple and powerful: these were our islands, we should have protected them, and we are going to take them back.

Mrs. Thatcher then proceeded to warn the Argentinians that there was a British nuclear submarine near the islands and, should any invading force enter the waters within a three-mile radius, the submarine would take aggressive action. Convinced of Mrs. Thatcher's feint, the Argentinians halted any attempt to land forces by water. This created a temporary standoff and gave Britain three days to organize and mobilize its troops. The first wave of Argentinian troops remained on the islands, but no more arrived to support them.

Now, here's the clincher: *There was no nuclear submarine.* It was all a bluff. However, Thatcher delivered her story with such passion, clarity, and earnestness, and the rest of her story was so factually accurate, that she convinced the entire world Britain had a nuclear submarine near the Falklands and averted what had the potential to be a much more serious war.

In this regard, we all understand the power of stories, but often, as with the Thatcher story, they feel somewhat abstract, affecting us only in some distant way. For me, that was all about to change.

After I finished my first-year studies in the United Kingdom, I landed in America—in Wilmington, North Carolina, to be exact—where I continued studying psychology and communication. In 1992, some friends and I embarked on a three-week cross-country road trip from Wilmington to Los Angeles.

At the time, we didn't have a care in the world other than enjoying ourselves, touring the American countryside, and eventually experiencing the vibrant LA culture we'd heard so much about. However, when we arrived, LA was oddly quiet. Instead of tourist traps and street performers, we saw only empty streets. Instead of fancy convertibles and luxury cars, we saw only armored trucks.

As we learned, the narrative around an entire region can turn on a dime. None of us had paid any attention to the media as we traveled across the country, so we didn't know that as we neared LA, the jury in the Rodney King trial had reached its verdict, and the city had erupted into a full-blown riot.

I remember sitting outside of Echo Park and watching the rioters literally come to the end of our street, or later watching from a bar as curfew was imposed and the streets emptied. Truly, it was a bizarre time. Sometimes we only hear about stories like this, while other times our own stories intersect.

For this experience alone, I knew I was exactly where I wanted to be. Soon after, my dream of the LA story came true as I found my way into the film industry, LA's most cherished institution.

THE PASSION, PROFITABILITY, AND HAPPINESS INDEX

The intersection of education and real-world experience forever cemented the power of storytelling in my mind, scoring high on my passion, profitability, and happiness index:

- **Passion:** I'm passionate about using stories to sell ideas, and I can trace this passion to this once-in-a-lifetime experience.
- **Profitability:** Seeing events like this unfold provided a real-world education and set me up for my career.
- **Happiness:** In spite of the rioting and the conflicts, I was happy, with friends, and experiencing life.

Have you even been in a situation where your own personal or professional life crossed paths with a larger social event? If so, how did you respond?

FINAL TAKEAWAYS

In this chapter, I hope you learned a thing or two about marketing—chiefly, how to build a good strategy, how to integrate efforts, and how to price competitively. Before we dive into Chapter 6, here are my three biggest marketing takeaways:

1. Marketing happens before sales.
2. Successful marketing requires visibility and credibility.
3. It's all about the *why*.

Congratulations! You're well on your way to becoming a marketing master. Next, let's talk about sales.

NOW FOR SOME FUN

Guerilla marketing is an innovative, unconventional, and low-cost marketing technique aimed at obtaining maximum exposure for a brand, product, or service. What's the most fun guerilla marketing you have used or experienced?

Once you've given it some thought, share here:

http://www.exactlywhereyouwanttobe.com/marketing

CHAPTER 6

SALES IS NOT A DIRTY WORD

———

To me, job titles don't matter. Everyone is in
sales. It's the only way we stay in business.

—HARVEY MACKAY

Meet Torrey, owner of Sparkhouse.[20] This cool Californian company offers video marketing, advertising, and production, with particular expertise in filmmaking for the digital world.

For Sparkhouse, as with any creative service, proving your worth over a competitor's is challenging, and not only because of budget. The same concept can sell for wildly different prices with no noticeable difference in quality.

---

20 www.thesparkhouse.com

As an extra challenge, Sparkhouse's creative services are often sold via a third-party ad agency, affording them zero contact with the end client. This means Torrey and his team don't get a project brief, and they don't get to make a pitch. Compounding things, the advertising agency acts as a gatekeeper, deciding how much of a client's budget to allocate to video services like Torrey's.

With all these challenges, how does Torrey win such a high number of customers?

Torrey targets his sales at only twenty-eight people—specifically, the leaders of twenty-eight of the top marketing agencies in Southern California. While he may eventually expand to target seventy or more, these twenty-eight leaders give him more than enough business to grow Sparkhouse.

Torrey's approach is successful for two reasons. First, by targeting the leaders of top marketing agencies, Torrey masterfully leverages the benefits of working with an agency. After all, one amazing project for an agency all but guarantees you more business.

Second, Torrey succeeds because the leaders he targets buy into Torrey himself. He's high-energy, enthusiastic, and passionate. You can see the pride he takes in his craft, his love of putting together a new creative concept, and the thrill he gets from his work. Prospects, clients, and team members can feel this enthusiasm radiate from him, making Sparkhouse the no-brainer choice for these marketing agencies.

SALES IS A PERSONAL GAME

People buy from people they respect and believe in. However, what's true for marketing is also true for sales—you need visibility and credibility. No one will respect or believe in you if they don't know who you are or what you've done.

Torrey maintains high visibility by targeting a narrow list of prospects, and his credibility increases with every project he completes. Most people don't like selling, but as covered in Chapter 4, as a business owner, you're selling to everyone all the time. This isn't always easy considering that you must face constant rejection. Who enjoys that?

Many business owners list sales as their primary concern. Becoming a successful salesperson takes time, strategy, and practice, but it's worth it. Once you've developed this skill, however, your business will be poised to reap great rewards and could experience exponential growth.

The key is to avoid the same old tired and clichéd sales approaches. In fact, if you learn one thing from this chapter, it's this: avoid overused, sleazy used car sales tactics. Be personable and be real. If you can do this, then sales won't feel like such a dirty word.

When I speak at a business event or lecture at universities, inevitably, someone will ask, "What's the number one thing you need to be successful in business?" I often hear groans when I say it, but my top three answers are always: sales, sales, sales.

It's time to turn those groans into gratitude. After all, how else are you going to live your dream and get exactly where you want to be?

In this chapter, we're diving headfirst into sales. Along the way, I'll give you plenty of tools and actionable tips to improve your close rate and grow your business.

WHY IS SALES SO IMPORTANT?

The bald truth is that without sales, there's no revenue. Without revenue, there's no business.

If you're generating revenue but not profit, there are plenty of solutions. But if you're not generating revenue, then there's no dancing around it; you've got a sales problem.

Despite our misgivings about selling in a business environment, we humans sell constantly. We sell ideas and stories to our loved ones, our parents, and our partners. It sounds weird to say this since the term "sales" has taken on so many negative connotations, but there's nothing weird about it.

As a business owner, you must know how to sell. Chances as you're the primary salesperson—the rainmaker—for your company. You live your product, and as such, you know the intricacies of the industry, customers, and the competition better than any of your team members. With your in-depth knowledge and passion, you can discuss every aspect of your product or service confidently and convincingly.

However, no one is an island, and as your business grows, you won't have time to handle every sale yourself. You'll need to hire a sales team and take on the role of sales manager (more on that in Chapter 7). To get there, let's talk about how sales can grow your business.

There are essentially two sales methods, each with multiple variations. Whichever method you lean toward, remember that it's perfectly okay to deviate, tweak, and personalize that technique to suit your personality and business needs.

SALES METHOD #1

Action selling, challenger sales, spin selling, consultative selling—whatever you want to call these models—all have a map of what to do, in what order.

I'm going to do you a huge favor, save you a significant amount of time and money, and upset a lot of people who sell sales books and coaching services in the process. This type of sale is a simple four-point process:

1. Attract attention.
2. Arouse interest.
3. Develop desire.
4. Close the sale.

Here are the steps necessary to make this work:

1. Prequalify the target.
2. Approach.
3. Present and demonstrate.

4. Handle objections.
5. Close the sale.
6. Deliver or follow up.

All of these elements require you to develop and maintain relationships and cultivate trust. Great salespeople are great communicators. They build effective customer relationships by demonstrating appreciation, flexibility, and credibility. Let's explore each element of the sales process in greater detail.

PLANNING AND MANAGEMENT

For successful sales using this method, you have to prepare. This involves prospecting, prequalifying targets, and cultivating relationships. You'll need to identify your target market geographically, gain an understanding of customer preferences, and prepare marketing collateral, introductory offers, and samples. You'll also need to establish ways of getting in touch with the target's decision maker.

There are four key areas of knowledge you need:

- Yourself
- Your company
- The product
- The customer

What can you do to prepare for the sales interview?

- Research the customer.
- Research the product until you know it inside and out.
- Research existing relationships between your company and the customer.
- Know every step in your sales funnel.
- Understand objectives regarding other products for the same customer.
- Understand other objectives for the same product and customer.
- Ask questions to understand the client's needs.
- Ask more questions to find leads.
- Ask even more questions to stay in control of the interview.

As part of your preparation, be aware of these seven barriers to verbal and nonverbal communication that can inhibit your sales ability:

1. Slow greeting
2. Indifference
3. Personal appearance
4. Lack of knowledge
5. Distractions
6. Emotion
7. Competitive offerings

Overcome these barriers using the following:

- Enthusiasm—channel your inner Torrey
- Self-organization
- Silence—listen and observe
- Show interest and seek agreement
- Use questions to find out more
- Be sincere—show confidence and attentiveness
- Be knowledgeable
- Be honest and give praise where appropriate
- Remember names and faces
- Do not forget a customer's name
- Close the sale in a single final action

PRESENTING

There are five key things you need to do for a successful presentation:

- Explain benefits, not features.
- Keep the focus on the customer and their needs.
- Answer any objections and probe to make objections and answers specific.
- Put objections into perspective.
- Look for buying signals, close the sale, then keep quiet.

Once you've made the sale, get out of the sale situation as quickly as possible to avoid inadvertently making your newfound customers change their minds.

All of those sales strategies from the start of this section—such as action, challenger, or spin selling—all have their merits, but they are all built on this foundation. This is great news for you, since it means you can use this same foundation to build a sales process that works for your unique circumstances.

Remember, every sale is different. Build in some flexibility with your sales method. As long as you're authentic and honest, there is no one right or wrong method if the end result is a sale. All businesses I'm involved with use different methods, and even those using the aforementioned recognized methods apply them in different ways.

THE FUN STUFF

Got all that? Great, now it's time for some homework.

Write Out Your Sales Process

First things first. Don't worry, you can refine it later. Because you can't jump a prospect from qualification to closing, be sure to build in enough touchpoints so you can build a relationship and move them smoothly through the sales process.[21]

Your sales process might look something like this:

- Identify prospects on LinkedIn using the platform's advanced search feature.
- Reach out via LinkedIn.
- If no response, reach out again.
- After connecting, gather their email address and any other relevant information.
- Add the prospect to a four-week email drip campaign.
- Email a free whitepaper.
- Connect by phone and schedule a fifteen-minute call.
- During the fifteen-minute meeting, schedule a forty-five-minute face-to-face meet-up.
- At the meet-up, invite them to your office to try your product.
- After they've tried the product, ask if they're ready to buy it.

There you have it, your very own sales funnel!

---

21 Now, if your prospect immediately decides they love you and desperately need your product, they can leap right to the end of the process and let you close the sale without navigating through every touchpoint. This is always great news, but it's not the norm.

Create Scripts and Templates

Write out what needs to be said and done at each step—yes, even if you're already awesome at selling. Here's why:

- As you write, you'll see ways to improve.
- It provides consistency across multiple sales.
- Consistency lets you see what works and what needs further improvement.
- The more you define and build templates for the process, the quicker and more efficient every action becomes.

PUT IT ALL TOGETHER

Using the funnel, write out the exact advanced search criteria you would use on LinkedIn to establish likely prospects. Next, get ready to reach out by writing down the exact message you'll send. After that, determine how long you'll wait between your first and second contact attempts, and tailor your second message accordingly.

Complete each of the emails you want to use in your drip campaign, and then write out the script for your contact call. Soon, you'll be ready to meet in person. At this point, ask yourself what stages you still need to go through and what you still need to express.

Completing this task gives you a comprehensive sales process with enough flexibility for you to hone and refine until you optimize your results. Once it's perfect, you might even be able to sell your process to others.

SALES METHOD #2

Emotional sales. Like the first sales method, this approach also has multiple versions. One I particularly like is found in the book, *Pitch Anything: An Innovative Method For Presenting, Persuading, and Winning the Deal*, by Oren Klaff. As Klaff explains, great sales come from great communicators, communication is rooted in psychology, and psychology is rooted in the development of the brain. To show how this all works, *Pitch Anything* introduces the STRONG methodology:

- Setting the frame
- Telling the story
- Revealing the intrigue
- Offering the prize
- Nailing the hook point
- Getting a decision

Whether it's the *Pitch Anything* model or one of the others, the premise is the same. Use emotion to steer the conversation without worrying about navigating specific steps to close a sale. Understanding the emotions driving your customers at both the marketing and sales points is key. Here are six emotions:

1. **Fear:** If I don't decide now, I'll suffer.
2. **Greed:** If I decide now, I'll benefit.
3. **Altruism:** Deciding now helps others.
4. **Competition:** If I don't decide now, my competitors will outshine me.
5. **Smarts:** If I decide now, I'll look smart.
6. **Stupidity:** If I don't decide, I'll look stupid.

Fear is the most potent emotional driver in sales, but you need to recognize and understand all these emotions to regularly close sales.

TIPS AND TRICKS

There's so much conflicting advice out there that it can be overwhelming—and no matter what route you take, you will be applauded by some and derided by others.

Here's my best advice: Keep it simple, and don't try to fit your process into a standard mold. Figure out what's most effective for your business and stick with it. Here are some steps you can take to do exactly that.

1. Decide what you want to do and establish how you'll do it.

2. Write it down.

3. Try it.

4. Review it.

5. Refine it.

6. Repeat it.

By keeping your process simple and your objectives clear, you will develop a nuanced, practical understanding of the sales process that suits you and your business goals.

THE FOUR UNIVERSAL TRUTHS

We've already come a long way, but I get the feeling you still want a few more sales ideas. Here are four universal truths of successful business sales.

STOP SELLING, START HELPING

In the digital age, if a customer wants to find pricing, a testimonial, or information about your product, they can get it all online. They don't need you to sell to them; they need you and your sales team to *help* them. Help them find answers to their problems and help them make an informed decision. Research shows companies that help and educate their customers enjoy 47 percent larger purchases than companies who merely pitch.[22]

BUILD A SMART TECHNOLOGICAL FOUNDATION

When you're spending your time in sales, most of your time will be spent making calls, writing emails, and logging into a sales system. Therefore, optimizing these activities with the right technology maximizes productivity and ensures optimal resource usage. Sure, you can use a whiteboard or an Excel sheet to track sales, but you'll get better results from an online customer relationship management system, and some cost under $20 per month. The more you measure and automate, the better your sales will be.

22 The Annuitas Group.

SALES IS A SCIENCE, NOT AN ART

Sales isn't magic. With data readily available, you can track and gain insight into your sales process and use cold, hard facts to refine your process. If you're new to the science of sales, keep it simple. Start by tracking these key metrics:

- Average deal size
- Average sales cycle length
- Lead-to-deal conversion rate
- Calls per day
- Number of deals in progress

As always, once you get in the swing of things, you'll likely find other metrics to help you with your particular business needs.

GET PROSPECTS TO SAY "NO"

Most sales processes focus too heavily on making customers say "yes." This goes back to prequalifying prospects. Many deals fail to close because the prospect should never have been qualified to begin with. If a prospect doesn't have a firm answer for four out of these five variables, consider them unqualified and move on:

1. **Pain.** Does the customer have a pain point great enough to drive the need to change?

2. **Power.** Who is responsible for making the purchase?
3. **Money.** Does the prospect have a realistic budget?
4. **Process.** Do you know their entire buying process?
5. **Timeline.** Are they ready to purchase?

As we discussed in the last chapter, the clearer you know your top-tier customer profiles, the more effective your business will be, and the faster it will grow. It may feel wrong, but you're doing your business a service by being picky with who you sell to and who you don't.

KEY SALES METRICS

Want a little more motivation? Here are some key sales statistics you should be aware of.

First, let's look at how many contacts it takes to make a sale. The following data show the chance of closing a sale based on the number of your contacts (and, of course, this is an average, so it may be different for you).[23]

- First contact: 2 percent
- Second contact: 3 percent
- Third contact: 5 percent
- Fourth contact: 10 percent
- Fifth to twelfth contact: 80 percent

The numbers here are certainly very compelling. However, one look at the behavior of the average sales team tells us a different story.

- 48 percent never follow up with a prospect
- 25 percent make a second contact, then stop
- 12 percent make a third contact, then stop
- 10 percent contact a prospect more than three times

The numbers are clear. Want to increase your sales? Follow up with your prospects more than five times.

Finally, repeat business is another way to boost your bottom line.

- Repeat customers spend 33 percent more than new

---

23 These numbers are often quoted as being from The National Sales Executives Association. However, our research couldn't produce any evidence of such a group. Maybe the stats are just an online-perpetuated urban myth.

customers.[24]

- Referrals from repeat customers are 107 percent greater than noncustomers.
- It costs six times less to sell to an existing customer than to a prospect.
- Retaining current customers costs five times less than acquiring a new one.
- A 2 percent increase in customer retention is the equivalent of cutting costs by 10 percent.
- On average, businesses lose 10 percent of their customers.
- A 5 percent reduction in customer defection increases profits by 25 percent.

Now it's time for your moment of truth. Which group of professionals do you belong to? Are you part of the elite 10 percent who contact a prospect more than three times? Are you putting more effort into finding new customers than nurturing existing ones? Do you want to stay in touch with your existing customers but don't know how? You need a strategic sales plan, and you need it today.

SELLING IN HOLLYWOOD

When we last left off with my story, my friends and I were in LA with the Rodney King riots still in full swing. There we were, sitting outside the Cat & Fiddle on Sunset Boulevard watching the National Guard and their armored trucks roll by.

---

24 These numbers are printed in *Increasing Sales through Relationship Marketing*, by Juri Yoshida, but without further reference. Is this also fake news?

After this important moment in American cultural history had passed, it was time for us to settle in and establish ourselves—which, since we were in LA, meant getting into the movie business.

Soon, I was part of a distribution and production company in LA, visiting film festivals and operating for four weeks of the year out of an exorbitantly priced broom cupboard at the InterContinental Carlton Cannes Hotel. We spent far too much money there, but the location was perfect. It was located right between some of the largest movie houses.

The focus of my company was on international film distribution. For me, success as a salesman meant many long nights stationed in front of a fax machine in the weeks leading up to the Cannes Film Festival. My goal was to set up three, twenty-minute meetings per hour with international film buyers to sell as many of our movies as possible. We represented around twelve movies across many mediums and distributed to as many countries as possible. Of those, we produced two or three ourselves.

Each meeting was the same. First, I would ask, "What kind of movie are you buying today?" Then, I would stop and listen to the prospect's answer.

Invariably, my answer was always, "I have a movie like that! Here's the flyer." How is it that I always had what the buyer was looking for? Well, for each movie we represented, we produced multiple flyers. One focused on the action, another on the romance, another on the comedy, and so on. That way, it didn't matter what the buyer was looking for. We had it.

THE PASSION, PROFITABILITY, AND HAPPINESS INDEX

Make no mistake, working in Hollywood producing, selling, and distributing films was absolutely where I wanted to be. It taught me a lot about the kind of professional I would become:

- **Passion.** Selling movies isn't easy. Yes, we were doing exciting work in a beautiful region of the world, but we also spent nearly two straight weeks in back-to-back, twenty-minute meetings selling our movies—and when we weren't in meetings, we were reviewing scripts.
- **Profit.** When done right, the movie business makes great profit. Even the awful movie called *One Missed Call* (2008), which was a remake of a Japanese horror movie and scored a well-deserved 0 percent on *Rotten*

Tomatoes, grossed $26.9 million on a $20 million budget.

- **Happiness.** There I was, sitting on the terrace of the InterContinental Carlton Cannes Hotel, sipping a glass of French champagne, reading scripts, and being surrounded by the most influential moviemakers of our time. Once, I sat across from George Lucas, totally oblivious until a swarm of about twenty paparazzi engulfed him.

Here's the moral of the story: sell like you mean it. Read people quickly, determine what they want, and connect with them authentically. Don't rely on tired sales methodologies. Instead, if you must, adopt any helpful strategies you see in them, but make your sales process your own.

FINAL TAKEAWAYS

See? Sales isn't so scary once you learn to embrace it and build a clear, repeatable process around it. In the next chapter, we'll talk about growing your operation. But for now, here are the three most important takeaways:

1. People buy from people.
2. Embrace sales. Embrace life. Show more enthusiasm than anyone else.
3. Find your own sales process and own it.

As we move on to building your own sales team, remember: you're already better at sales than you give yourself credit for. Trust your knowledge, live your passion, and channel those traits through a well-thought sales strategy.

TIME FOR SOME FUN

What is the story of your most successful sale? On a scale of 1–10, how much enthusiasm did you exude at the time?

Once you've given it some thought, share here:

http://www.exactlywhereyouwanttobe.com/sales

CHAPTER 7

NO MAN IS AN ISLAND

———

If everyone is moving forward together,
then success takes care of itself.

—HENRY FORD

Meet Brian Olson, the second-generation owner of "the bugman"—a leading termite and pest control company.[25] Brian is happiest when he can make both customers and team members happy—creating raving fans in the process.

Back in 1958, when California was covered in orange groves and eucalyptus trees, Brian's father, Herb Olson, had a vision for a service company. When Brian took over the reins from his father, Brian performed every function in the business. He learned by doing, and that has propelled the bugman onto the list of the national top pest

---

25 http://www.thebugman.com

control industry's one hundred largest companies for the sixth year in a row.

Growing the team and growing sales is where he excels. As with most business owners, Brian knows that sales are the wings of his company. Unlike many other business owners, however, Brian has developed through three business metamorphosis steps (without being stung).

First, Brian learned how to sell. More than selling, he learned how to listen to the needs of his customers and offer the service they need.

Second, Brian developed a team of great salespeople. How do I know they are great? Because some of them have been there for over two decades, and because they are all high-performing salespeople who are well remunerated.

Third is the hardest part. Brian is putting in a sales manager to keep the sales team running strong. This is one of the hardest things for a business owner to do. After all, there really are only two options for finding a sales manager: hiring externally or promoting from within.

I've seen companies close their doors because of the time and cost involved in hiring a highly paid sales manager (and shouldn't all well-performing sales managers be well paid?). Luckily, Brian already had a high-performing team member interested in the sales manager role.

You may realize this posed a problem. After all, why take one of your best salespeople out of the field so they can manage others? The best salespeople do not always become the best sales managers—not to mention the short-term dip in sales during the training process.

With careful planning, the right support, and a plan in place, this kind of transition is not only possible, but also potentially very successful. Just ask Brian. Whatever stage of sales, sales management, or placing a sales manager you are in, this chapter will guide you through some universal truths.

SALES MANAGEMENT

How do you motivate your team and keep them accountable? Great sales management can lead to great sales results, but you've got to earn it. It may not be easy, but it's absolutely worthwhile.

HIRING

Building the right sales team is crucial to your success, so establish a method that helps you hire well. Outstanding salespeople need self-motivation, the right outlook on life, and a readiness to live by your company values. Hire people with direct experience selling in both your industry and at the volumes you're expecting.

TRAINING

Once you've hired your team, you need to train them. Here, it's important to keep in mind that training isn't some one-and-done effort. All of your team members—but especially your sales team—should constantly be learning new things and improving their knowledge base and approach.

Take an active role in your team's training. Not only do you know your product better than anyone else, but you also have an innate understanding of the *what* and the *how* of your business, not to mention who you're selling to and the pain points your product resolves. Your ability to share this knowledge is invaluable to improving your team's knowledge and performance.

Everything we learned about sales in Chapter 6 is going to be relevant to the people you work with on your sales team. Use that chapter as the basis of your sales manual, the document that lists every feature and benefit of your product, details the sales process, and answers every question a prospect could ask. I promise, the more attention you pay to this, the more it will pay off in future sales training.

HUNT VAMPIRES

The sales vampire is the person who isn't performing well and is sucking energy from you, your business, and the customer. Identify them and remove them.[26] It might sound harsh, but you want only the best service for your customers and prospects.

Using a scale of one to ten, how vampirish is each member of your sales team? If anyone scores above a seven, meaning they're closer to Dracula than they are to Van Helsing, get rid of them this Friday afternoon.

OPERATING SYSTEM

What is the process to acquire new customers, and what is the process to earn repeat business? What steps does your team follow, and how do you measure results? Establish an operating system that meets the following objectives:

1. Teams report in a simple, efficient manner.
2. Your sales team is accountable.

---

26 Yes, I understand that firing is a tough proposition and can be a little tough to stomach. Don't worry. We'll address this topic in greater detail in Chapter 10.

3. You openly encourage and reward your team.

Which customer relationship management (CRM) system do you use? Does it suit your needs? Don't skimp on CRM software. It's integral to the sales process.

SALES FUNDAMENTALS

With your fundamentals, it's not about the product, but about the actual sales elements. Regardless of how much experience your team has, there's always room for improvement. Verbal and nonverbal communication can be refined, and ever-changing technologies and societal niceties mean constant learning for your team. Make use of third-party training as much as you can to keep your team fresh.

THE SALES TEAM

Let's be clear: while hiring a full-time, in-house sales team is a viable option, it isn't the only one. Consider independent sales reps or representative agencies. If, like many business leaders, you want to keep your sales team in-house, here are six traits to look for when hiring salespeople:

1. **Emotional intelligence.** It's not only about reading the sales manual, but also about reading the room.
2. **Work ethic.** Sales is a 24/7/365 job. Candidates need to be prepared to dive in and get the job done, whatever it takes.
3. **Successes.** Don't focus only on past sales success. Any victory matters, from sports to academics.
4. **Creativity.** People with creative flair can help you and customers find solutions.
5. **Entrepreneur's spirit.** Sales is like running a business; you need to think on your toes and focus on offering solutions.
6. **Competitive.** Sales is a competition—with your teammates, yourself, and rival companies. Find people who hate to lose and won't stop until they win.

If a candidate embodies these six traits but is still a little rough around the edges, give them a shot. They don't have to be perfect, but they do have to be trainable.

FOUR FUNDAMENTALS OF SALES SUCCESS

The key to business success is sales, right? To an extent, that is true; the greater your sales, the better you're doing. However, as the forward-thinking business owner you are, you don't want mere short-term gains. You want sustainable, long-term success. The following four fundamentals will help you get there.

KEY PERFORMANCE INDICATORS

You have to measure something before you can improve it. It's not just the number of sales, but the factors that lead to sales. Look at your sales funnel. Measure as many of the steps as possible. The more actions you measure, the easier it becomes to identify what *needs* to be measured. Examine the closure rates of each key performance indicator to assess which ones need refining and to predict future sales.

So with that in mind, here's the literal million-dollar question: What are *you* measuring?

MOTIVATION

Understand what motivates your sales team. Get to know them on a more personal level, and you'll know how to effectively motivate them.

While it's important to be authentic and not work too much off a script for this, here are a few insightful questions you can ask your team members:

- What aspects of your job do you most like, and which do you prefer to delegate?
- How much time do you want to devote to work?
- How much and what type of vacation do you want?
- How much money do you want to make?
- What intangible rewards excite you?
- What are your spiritual beliefs?
- What do you do outside of the office?
- What personal achievements drive you?
- Do you have any humanitarian interests?
- What family commitments are important to you?
- When do you want to retire?

Again, these are just starting points, so don't be afraid to throw a few curveballs in there. You'll be surprised at what you can learn.[27]

FRIENDLY COMPETITION

Salespeople are competitive. They have to be. So, utilize that passion for winning. Run competitions, bonuses, and rewards programs. Alternatively, consider subscribing to one of the team member reward services available online. Whatever you decide, make sure it's simple enough not to detract from selling well, and make sure it actually

---

27 Sound familiar? It should. These are the same questions you answered for your personal vision in Chapter 2. You *did* remember to answer those, right?

motivates and incentivizes. Finally, don't forget to deliver any promised rewards on time.

ACCOUNTABILITY

Hold your team accountable. Plan for daily, twice-weekly, or weekly status updates, and give feedback to your team. Be honest and focus on the good and bad points, and remember to account for seasonal fluctuations and reciprocal factors. The frequency of feedback meetings depends on your industry and the size of your company, as does whether meetings are virtual or in person. Figure out what works for you. And never, ever miss a meeting.

Once you start holding regular meetings, ask yourself: are you really holding your team accountable? It's not much help if you're simply going through the motions.

FOUR KEY SALES METRICS

If you see sales start to drop, know that it's not uncommon, particularly if you're just beginning to scale up. There could be a number of factors, including:

- New team members
- A change in lead quality
- A change in management

- Packaging
- Pricing
- Website issues

This is why metrics are so important, as they help you quickly establish where things are falling off in the sales process. For instance, if most of your reps are falling off in the same area, they probably aren't to blame. If a particular rep is inexplicably excelling, it could be they are awesome at sales, or it could also be they are talented sandbaggers or cherry pickers. Investigate all available data before jumping to conclusions.

In that pursuit, here are four key metrics:

NUMBER OF OPEN OPPORTUNITIES PER REP

How many open opportunities is each rep working on at one time, and how many new opportunities should each rep be assigned per month? Your reps need a sufficient flow of new opportunities so they have a steady flow of work, but not so many that they're overwhelmed and their performance or customer service suffers.

Establish how many opportunities your best sales reps deal with on average. Does the number vary by deal size, customer type, or segment? At what point did your people start to get overwhelmed? Establishing this figure lets you see whether you need to qualify more leads or increase the size of your sales team.

NUMBER OF CLOSED OPPORTUNITIES

Measure the total closed *won* and closed *lost* opportunities for each rep. They should be closing a minimum number of opportunities per month, win or lose.

If they aren't doing this, figure out why. Are they light on deals? Are they not closing effectively? Are they not updating the sales system? Put on your detective hat and find out.

THE MONETARY DEAL SIZE

Measure the average value of your closed *won* deals. This lets you easily spot when things fall outside the normal range. For example, you can flag deals that are particularly larger than normal so they receive special attention. You can also spot decreases in average deal sizes, which may indicate reps are either giving deeper discounts or are spending too much energy pursuing smaller fish.

WIN RATE

Measure the total number of closed opportunities and the total number of wins in a given period. Divide the total closed *won* opportunities by the *total closed* (won and lost) opportunities to find your win rate. A high win rate is good; a low win rate is not. Knowing your win rate lets you hone your sales system. For instance, a high win rate may indicate that you need to raise your prices or generate more leads.

To improve your win rate, identify the two most problematic areas in your sales process.

HOW TO IDENTIFY THE BEST SALESPEOPLE

Before we wrap up this chapter, let's talk about recruitment. Based on available data, the average cost of a bad hiring decision is six times the base salary for a sales rep and fifteen times the base salary for a sales manager.[28]

In other words, you've got to know what kind of person you want to hire, since a mistake can be costly. The following are eight characteristics of the ideal salesperson and how to unearth them during an interview.

---

28 Society for Human Resources Management.

COACHABILITY

A great sales rep has to listen, learn, and adapt. They need to be responsive to coaching, which is a powerful driver of sales success.

Interview Tactics

Ask your sales candidate, "Tell me about a time when you knew you were right but still had to follow direction."

At the end of the interview, gauge their self-awareness by asking, "How do you think you did?" Then, deliver your feedback and gauge their response. At follow-up interviews, do they act on this feedback in a positive way?

DELIVER CLEAR EXPLANATIONS

Great salespeople can convey complex information simply and clearly. All the product knowledge in the world is useless if the candidate can't deliver it in an easily understandable way. Your salespeople need to break down complex matters into clear messages and straightforward action items that make the prospect feel informed and in control.

Interview Tactics

Ask your sales candidate to tell the story of why they want to change roles or of a key mistake they've made. If they cannot succinctly convey a story, they won't excel in sales.

Ask the candidate to explain the market they're currently selling to or to explain the last product they sold.

CAN THEY WRITE?

A large part of any job in sales involves writing: cold emails, warm leads, follow-ups, proposals, contracts, etc. Their writing ability indicates their professionalism and reflects on your company. You can expect a high-performing sales person to communicate at an eleventh- to twelfth-grade level, while an underachiever communicates at an eighth- to ninth-grade level.

Interview Tactics

Ask the candidate to write an outreach email for one of your products.

Ask the candidate to prepare a proposal and bring it to the interview.

PROCESS-DRIVEN

Salespeople manage multiple leads simultaneously, each with many touchpoints across a long sales funnel. The only way to manage that workload effectively is to be process-driven.

Interview Tactics

Ask your candidate, "In your current role, what metrics do you use to track your progress and goals?"

Ask, "How do you organize your day, week, or year? Please share an example."

PERSEVERANCE

One of the most overlooked characteristics of great salespeople is their perseverance. The most successful sales reps always follow up, whereas the mediocre ones don't bother to follow up or simply give up too easily.

Interview Tactics

Ask your sales candidate, "How would you approach a sales situation in which a qualified prospect is not answering your email?"

Ask, "How many times would you reach out to a prospect who isn't answering your calls?"

ACTIVE LISTENING

The best salespeople listen attentively and use an economy of words. They ask open-ended questions that encourage the prospect to speak more.

Interview Tactics

Take long pauses. Does the candidate rush to fill the silence, or do they wait for you to speak?

Take note of what kind of questions they ask you. Do they ask open-ended questions that invite you to speak?

MONEY TALK

Salespeople have to be confident talking about money. There's no way to avoid that conversation. Whether a prospect is a solid lead depends in part on their budget. So the sooner a rep has the money talk, the sooner they can establish whether a prospect is a good fit.

Interview Tactics

Ask your candidate, "Can you tell me what salary you're currently on and what you require for this position?"

Ask, "What's the most expensive purchase you've ever made?"

PREPARATION

Salespeople must be prepared at every stage of the sales process to be effective.

Interview Tactics

Establish whether the candidate has prepped for the interview by asking, "What do you know about me?"

Establish exactly what you need your sales person to do, what you want them to sell, the value of the sale, and your typical sales cycle. Then find people who are familiar with all of those aspects. Don't hire someone who excels at selling a $1,000 product if yours is worth $100,000. Don't hire someone who excels at selling in New York if you sell in the Alaskan wilderness.

BACK IN THE UK

After a fun run in the film business, I ended up back in the UK, where I earned my MBA. I left academia overqualified and underexperienced and began my working life at a small business selling remanufactured print consumables from a barn on a farm in rural Berkshire.

Down on the farm, I learned the art of selling. Every day, I'd reach out to fifty new businesses by cold-calling on the phone, walking into office buildings, and by faxing messages (occasionally emailing them, though it was kind of early for anyone to have an email address at the time). By the evening, I'd be sitting in a local pub with my boss, sipping on a pint and reflecting on my day. Eventually, I was headhunted and went to work for a major technology company, where I headed up marketing in Eastern Europe and the Middle East.

My employers initially based me in Paris, but when I pointed out that Paris wasn't in Eastern Europe or the Middle East, they gave me a free hand to relocate anywhere. So, first I spent an amazing few years in Prague, and then I moved to Dubai.

One of my company's major sales initiatives was called "surround the customer." Think about it. If you're selling to a prospective customer and everyone they take advice from also recommends your product, you're in a very strong position. Long before the days of social media, we played this out with a high-value business-to-business sale, although it would have worked equally well in a consumer sale.

When I landed in Dubai as head of marketing, my office mate was head of sales, and we both reported to different people. After a particularly bad day, we decided to get away for a while. So, just forty-eight hours later, we found ourselves in Phuket, Thailand, eager to begin a five-day vacation in the middle of the workweek. We checked voicemails and emails every morning and evening, and spent the intervening time adventuring, relaxing, and experiencing everything Thailand had to offer.

The kicker? Nobody ever knew we had left Dubai.

THE PASSION, PROFITABILITY, AND HAPPINESS INDEX

From selling remanufactured print consumables to high-stakes sales in Dubai, I learned a lot about what drives a good sales team:

- **Passion.** We liked what we were doing, but too much time even at a job you love can burn you out. Our trip to Thailand was just what we needed to refocus our efforts.

- **Profitability.** Even though the head of sales and the head of marketing were enjoying themselves in Thailand, other people—our sales team—were landing sales and getting business for the company.
- **Happiness.** Thai food, diving, and riding elephants. Being paid to hang out in Thailand was pretty cool.

Here's the moral of the story. It's one thing to build a sales team, but it's another thing to trust them. Being more effective both as a business leader and a salesperson doesn't always mean working harder or putting in longer hours. In fact, sometimes it means the exact opposite.

THREE TAKEAWAYS

By now, you should have some ideas on why a strong sales team matters and how you can find and empower the best people for your business. Here are my three biggest takeaways:

1. Your sales team doesn't need to be full-time internal team members.
2. Hire the best salespeople you can afford.
3. Keep your sales team accountable.

As we move on to the next chapter, remember that having a good support system doesn't only help for sales. Your job as a business leader is to focus on what you love and what you do best. For everything else, bring in the pros.

NOW FOR SOME FUN

What is the best incentive you have experienced to motivate a salesperson or team?

Once you've given it some thought, share here:

http://exactlywhereyouwanttobe.com/salesmanagement

CHAPTER 8

DO WHAT YOU LOVE, OUTSOURCE THE REST

If you deprive yourself of outsourcing and your competitors do not, you're putting yourself at a disadvantage.

—LEE KUAN YEW

Meet Crystal Williams of RxReins.[29] She started as a receptionist, worked her way up, and eventually took over, driving the company forward to new heights. The business revolves around marketing, sales, underwriting, and administration. If you measure these tasks, it's clear that administration takes the longest time and requires the most labor. However, administration is not Crystal's passion.

---

29 www.rxreins.com

Within the last year, Crystal has negotiated an M&A—mergers and acquisitions—that added her business to a group of companies with symbiotic advantages. While this afforded her many opportunities, including capital and expertise, a key advantage was being able to outsource all her administration tasks to another company within the group. This freed up key team members who were then able to move into roles within marketing and sales.

Crystal spent a few months thoroughly documenting all of the required administration processes before she handed the job over to the outsourcing company. She was also able to improve and refine her processes and reduce fixed and variable costs. As a result, her business is thriving, she's closer to where she wants to be, and she's spending far more time on her passion.

How much could you do if you only did what you love? Are there any areas of your business that would be more efficient if you weren't doing them? Where should your focus be? Have you ever consciously asked yourself what parts of your business you like doing and which you don't?

If you don't like doing accounts, for example, you don't have to. You can easily hire someone at $15 to $25 per hour to do it for you. In fact, with the abundance of new technology, you can hire remote employees or freelancers. You could actually outsource every element of your business if you wanted to. In this chapter, we'll explore the ins and outs of outsourcing and how it can help your business.

WHY OUTSOURCE?

Business owners tend to do everything, which is fine for a small, young business, but it isn't practical as you grow. The business becomes dependent on you, and you're not focusing on your passion—the areas in which you excel and care most about. Instead, you're filling many roles, from purchasing office supplies and vending machines to HR matters, fixing the plumbing, and emptying the trash. That isn't going to get you where you want to be.

FOCUSING ON YOUR STRENGTHS

In Chapter 4, we talked about focusing on what you do best. In fact, I even had you list the top three most valuable positions you have within your company. Still have that list? Why not give it another look? I'll hang tight while you remind yourself.

If you're struggling to identify your top three positions, make a list of everything you do. Estimate how much money each item brings into your business over a defined period. Then, give yourself a rating, from one to ten, for how good you are at each item. Using the same scale, jot down how much you enjoy each activity. After this, you should be able to identify the two or three most important roles based on their value to your business and their value to you.

FOUR REASONS TO OUTSOURCE

It makes sense for you to focus on a few important roles and outsource or hire staff to take care of everything else. On occasion, you may even have to outsource jobs that you excel at. There are essentially four reasons to outsource:

- You are unable to focus.
- You can't do it.
- You don't want to do it.
- You don't have time to do it.

These reasons might sound over simplistic at first blush. However, as we've already learned throughout this book, the greatest strengths and weaknesses in any business are often rooted in simple causes.

WHAT'S THE DIFFERENCE BETWEEN AN EMPLOYEE AND AN INDEPENDENT CONTRACTOR?

It's important to understand the difference between an employee and an independent contractor (IC), if for no other reason than to avoid costly legal consequences. Let's break it down:

- **An independent contractor** operates under a business name, frequently their given name. They may have their own workforce and will invoice for work completed. An IC will have their own tools and systems and will likely have more than one client.
- **An employee** performs duties dictated by the company, usually works only for one employer, rarely operates external to the business, and is given training for the role within the company.[30]

Whatever your business relationship with others, it's important that you and the contractor/employee are on the same page as to their role, duties, and compensation structure.

---

30 Up to this point in the book, you may have noticed that I've generally avoided the word "employee." There's nothing especially wrong with the word, but it feels a little stuffy and formal compared to more inclusive terms like "team member." That said, here we're talking about legal business terms, so the formal "employee" will have to do.

DOES IT REALLY MATTER?

It absolutely matters that you clearly define your working relationship with your contractor/employee. Misclassification of an individual as an independent contractor when they're actually an employee can carry a number of costly legal consequences.

There's no actual test to determine whether an individual is an IC or an employee under the Fair Labor Standards Act in the United States. However, here are some questions and guidelines that should work as a foundation for both US-based companies and firms abroad:

- Is what you're outsourcing a critical part of your product or service?
- How long do you plan to work with that person?
- What is the amount of alleged contractor's investment in facilities and equipment?
- What type and how much control do you have over this person?
- What is the individual's profit and loss?
- How successful would the contractor be based on their own initiative and judgment?
- To what degree is your contractor's business organization independent of yours?

These questions are just meant to get you started. At the end of the day, this is not a place you want to cut corners. Make sure you have the most accurate legal guidelines available for where you do business, and clearly communicate your business relationship to your independent contractor.

BENEFITS OF ICS

There are many potential benefits to contracting freelancers instead of hiring employees. Usually, it comes down to three things:

- Lower labor cost
- Reduced liability
- Flexibility

Another crucial benefit is that you can hire the right person for the right role as needed. Often, freelancers have many years of experience, and by the nature of their job, they're adaptable, so you don't need to train them. This can make your offering even more valuable to customers.

POTENTIAL DRAWBACKS OF HIRING ICS

Working with independent contractors isn't always a smooth ride. Be aware of the potential for the following drawbacks:

- You lose some control over how work is completed.
- You can request repeat work from the same freelancer, but if they are good, they'll get booked up quickly.
- They don't have to be loyal to your business.
- Unless specified in your contract, any copyright will be owned by the freelancer.

Now that you've got the full picture, it should be much easier to avoid some of these pitfalls.

DEFINING ROLES

What's the difference between an independent contractor, a freelancer, and a consultant? While all three can work for your company on a project-by-project basis, and although the terms are often used interchangeably, there are some subtle differences.

- **Independent contractors** usually work on-site, completing projects for one client at a time under a direct contract with either your business or a third party. You may want to use independent contractors repeatedly or over a longer period of time. Independent contractors generally have professional qualifications and are frequently found in bookkeeping, engineering, photography, IT, technical services, real estate, sales, driving, plumbing, and similar roles.

- **Freelancers** typically work with multiple clients simultaneously, usually remotely. They tend to work directly with your company under a contract or agreed-upon terms. Freelancers are often used on a one-off basis. Some have professional qualifications, while others do not. You'll commonly find freelancers in journalism, writing, programming, software development, graphic design, and songwriting.

- **Consultants** deliver expert advice and guidance to multiple clients at a time. They can be remote or on-site and work directly with your company or via a third party. They usually require a strong contract and have deep professional skills. You'll commonly find them in financial planning, strategic planning, marketing, research, training, business planning, and commercial law sectors.

While it can sometimes be difficult keeping all the terminology straight, the good news is that with a greater variety of working relationships comes a better ability to fill your business needs.

FINDING THE RIGHT INDEPENDENT CONTRACTOR

If you decide you don't need to hire an employee just yet but still need to get a job done, you need an independent contractor. But how do you find the right one?

BUILD LONG-TERM RELATIONSHIPS

Once you've worked with your IC, enjoyed the experience, and found that they added value, clearly explain you will likely have more work for them down the road.

WHERE DO YOU ADVERTISE?

There are countless firms and online channels available for advertising your need for a freelancer. However, you may not want to advertise for freelancers where your prospects or customers might see it. Although attitudes are changing, there are still some negative connotations regarding hiring freelancers. Maybe online freelance directories are a better option, where you can reach out to suitable independent contractors.

KNOW WHAT YOU'RE LOOKING FOR

The clearer you've defined and communicated your own needs, the more likely you'll find a freelancer who's a good fit for your company:

- Do you have a clear scope of work you need the freelancer to perform?
- Do you have a firm budget for this work?
- What's the timeframe?
- What skills or experience does the contractor need?
- Do you have a list of negative criteria that would disqualify someone?

Compile a list answering all of these questions so all the information is readily available to all interested parties when you start reaching out.

START THE SEARCH

If you can, seek recommendations from customers, advisors, family, friends, and other people you trust. Utilize online resources like LinkedIn, or reach out to freelance contractor sites and find one that works for you. Depending on the job you're looking to outsource, you may be able to cut costs by working with a freelancer site that has people around the globe, essentially offshoring your work. You can also post your job on freelance job boards. However you choose to do this, make sure you provide all of the information you gathered from the previous section.

THE POWER OF THREE

You don't necessarily want to work with only one freelancer. If the project scope allows, bring in three freelancers. Just remember to set clear project parameters, detailing total cost, timeframe, and expected duties.

First, brief all three fully. Then, at a later date, review their work objectively. Ascertain which of the three you'd most like to work with. Document your decision. Similarly, document who you'd least like to work with and who you'd like to have as a backup in case your first choice becomes unavailable.

THE LIST

As you experience growth and need to do more outsourcing, you must stay organized. Keep a real-time list of what can be outsourced to whom and their contact information. Keep records of which freelancer is doing what for you, their rate, where they excel, and other similar criteria.

AUTOMATING FREELANCERS

If you're continually using freelancers and ICs, it makes sense to automate the process as much as possible. Set up an automated system or email templates that you can use to request or brief freelancers over and over again.

Streamlining how you take delivery of freelance work and building a robust auditing procedure reduces cost, improves efficiency, and ensures your reputation doesn't suffer. Design rigorous quality control procedures and set high standards for your freelancers. Doing so will benefit everyone.

Freelancer payment needs to be simple, efficient, and timely. You want to keep the best freelancers, and to do that you need to be a good partner. Simplify the payment process, set out the invoicing parameters, and pay invoices early. The smaller the freelancer/IC, the more dependent they are on payment. At my companies, for example, we have a dedicated email address to which freelancers send their invoices. This feeds directly into our accounts payable program, which then reminds us when to approve and pay invoices.

MANAGING FREELANCERS

As we've discussed, there's a difference between the level of control you have over employees and freelancers. This also differs by country. Technically, if you overmanage an independent contractor, you could open yourself to the risk of miscategorization. This could be costly. However, there's still an active role you need to play in the relationship. Here are some tips:

- Set a clear brief in writing, complete with examples and templates for clarity and efficiency.
- Set a clear expectation that the freelancer is expected to confirm receipt of each new project in a timely fashion.
- Check in with the freelancer for updates at regular intervals.
- Ensure you've given the freelancer everything they need to complete the project to a high standard.
- Let the freelancer know they can communicate any questions, problems, or concerns to you.
- Treat the best freelancers well. Outside of the project level, work to build a lasting professional relationship with them. Periodically reach out if there's the potential for a project coming up that you want to involve them in, and show your appreciation for their past efforts.

As you can see from Crystal's example, it really is possible to outsource any element of your business that you don't enjoy. You can find someone who loves doing everything you don't want to, and you'll build a better business in the process.

PERSONAL OUTSOURCING

This chapter wouldn't be complete if we didn't talk about personal outsourcing too. But what does personal outsourcing mean?

Business owners and entrepreneurs are busy people, and we always want more. As I write this, I have a great team that has worked around my home for a decade—a personal shopper who knows how to cut costs for a lot of the items I need, and another specialist who washes my car in the driveway.

Look at your personal vision. Remember, it's not all about money; it's about time too. Know what your time is worth and see if you can outsource some of those necessities to other specialists, so you can spend more time getting where you want to be. As a certain little sister sang, "Let it go, let it go, and run with the wind and sky."[31]

---

31 I'm sure many of you reading this book are parents, so it probably goes without saying that this little bit of insight comes from the modern Disney hit, *Frozen*.

ON WORK/LIFE INTEGRATION

Many business owners ask me how they can achieve a better work/life balance. Frankly, I'd hoped that term died with the 1980s. As we covered before, in the digital age, we shouldn't bother ourselves with work/life balance, but rather with work/life *integration*. Nowadays, you don't have to be in the office from nine to five. With so much technology available, we can go to the gym, go to Disneyland, or just about anywhere else and still be connected to our businesses. If a client needs to meet outside of regular hours, we can connect remotely and make it work. Take a look outside right now. I bet there's somebody walking their dog while attending a conference call.

How much time do you spend each day commuting to and from the office? Do you actually *need* to commute every day? Could you save time by communicating remotely? Today, it's common for people to attend meetings virtually. Surely you've been on a conference call and heard dogs barking, children playing, road noises, pigs, parrots—all the sounds of life going on while others are hard at work.

That said, remember your vision. You know what's important to you and where you want to be. You don't need work/life integration 24/7. Keep your goals firmly in mind and know when to shut down your work life and dedicate your time to personal matters.

A NEW COUNTRY, A NEW VENTURE

By 1999, I'd lived and worked in LA, Paris, Prague, and Dubai. Each locale brought me new success and rich experiences, but I decided it was time to break out on my own again. So, I launched NettResults, a Dubai-based integrated marketing and PR company specializing in servicing technology clients. Most of our work involved traditional public relations efforts, which meant a lot of press releases.

PR is a low-entry business. All you need to know is which journalists to reach out to and how to do so, which we accomplished with nothing more than a phone and a media list. We covered nine core countries and had very few competitors at the time, but we did have to keep track of hundreds of Arabic and English-speaking journalists and editors. We managed this by having two employees call every entry on our media list every week to find out if each journalist or editor was still with the same publication and whether their contact details were still relevant.

Eventually, when the quality was high enough, we purchased a subscription to a Middle Eastern media list, which was automatically updated for us. This saved a huge amount of time and freed up our two employees to make more meaningful contributions to our business.

This made my business far more efficient. The company we outsourced the media list to had many people updating the list in real time, so we learned about changes soon after they happened. This way, when a client asked us about someone, we would look in our database and impress them by always having up-to-date and relevant information.

THE PASSION, PROFITABILITY, AND HAPPINESS INDEX

It felt good to be striking out on my own again. Getting any new venture started can often be a chore, but because I always had an eye on exactly where we wanted to be, we were soon seeing the exact growth and results I'd envisioned:

- **Passion.** Our office no longer had to contend with the mind-numbing job of updating databases.
- **Profitability.** Our whole office was now directly involved with marketing and media relations, and we were impressing more clients than ever—which led to greater profit.
- **Happiness.** You could feel the vibe in the office, the constant hum of productivity and people doing what they loved.

The moral of the story is don't bang your head against the wall with work that can be done cheaper and more effectively by someone else. Not only do you save time, money, and emotional capital, you often end up looking better in the eyes of your client.

THREE TAKEAWAYS

I know that outsourcing can feel like a big risk. You might worry that you're giving up control or risking a drop in quality. As with so many of the concepts we've discussed throughout this book, it's all about a process. Define what you want, communicate it to your IC or freelancer, and focus on what you're best at.

Here are my three biggest takeaways:

- If you don't like it, outsource.
- Let it go.
- Integration, not balance.

There you have it, outsourcing demystified. However, as we'll learn in the next chapter, while businesses of all sizes are accustomed to farming out labor, sometimes it's better to go with a more permanent solution.

NOW FOR SOME FUN

What methods or processes do you employ to find, motivate, keep, and have the best results from freelancers?

Once you've given it some thought, share here:

http://exactlywhereyouwanttobe.com/outsourcing

CHAPTER 9

IF YOU CAN'T OUTSOURCE, HIRE

———

Slow to hire, quick to fire.

—UNATTRIBUTED

Meet Allan Stone, CEO of Intelitics.[32] The Intelitics platform offers global publishers and advertisers an advanced, user-friendly, data-driven multiplatform that allows them to engage in meaningful, mutually beneficial revenue opportunities.

To keep up with Intelitics's growth, Allan knew he needed to hire new team members, but he couldn't find the right people. He tried recruitment websites, LinkedIn, networking opportunities, and other channels, but

32 http://intelitics.com

candidates who exhibited the right combination of technological insight and advanced marketing were nowhere to be found.

Frustrated but determined, Allan tried a new approach, one that might resonate with his target team members a little better. First, he put his phone on a selfie stick and shot a short recruiting video describing the job requirements and his idea of the ideal candidate. Since he was using video, he also took the opportunity to show off the office's foosball table and cool meeting rooms. In doing so, he increased his company's credibility and better engaged with his target audience.

Allan paired his online recruiting video with an application that asked basic but targeted questions. For example, to find out whether a recruit was technologically aware, the application asked for the make and model of the applicant's phone and their LinkedIn and Facebook URLs. The form was connected to an internal system that alerted Allan to new respondents and allowed him to sort them into batches so he could respond in a timely manner. It also allowed Allan to sort applicants into lists so he could sift out those who did not answer all the questions or provided information outside the set parameters.

After six months of struggling to find the right person, Allan made a hire with his new recruiting system in less than six weeks.

Have you ever had trouble finding the right recruits? Do you find recruiting takes too much time away from other areas of the business? Have you ever regretted making a hire?

If so, you're not alone. However, if we can take one lesson from Allan's story, it's that recruiting is actually a sales process. In effect, you're selling the vision of your company and the idea of why someone should join your team. When you look at it that way, the road forward becomes instantly simpler.

HIRING IN ANY ECONOMY

Hiring today is tough. In 2008, after so many people lost their jobs, recruiting was easy. There was an abundance of talent looking for employment, and you could take your pick. Today, either those people have found jobs or their circumstances have changed.

Beyond family and friends, the best hires are often those recommended by someone in your business network. Knowing this, here's my advice: focus less on spending huge sums on recruitment agencies, LinkedIn posts, and advertising, and focus more on networking and building long-term connections.

When hiring, work to fill a role that requires a specific skill set or qualifications. That way, a portion of your targeting is already complete. Regardless of the necessary skills, you're also looking for someone you can trust, and someone whose thinking aligns with our own. This may be why close friends and family members are increasingly finding themselves in business with each other.

Shifting attitudes have further complicated things. Well-educated people are less motivated by positions in the traditional workforce. To persuade recruits to join their team, employers have to compete on several fronts to prove they're the best in the market.

Even with this approach, recruiting is rarely easy. If you are experiencing problems, it's most likely due to one of the following four factors:

1. Lack of clarity surrounding the role
2. A weak flow of candidates
3. Lack of confidence in your own ability to pick the right candidate
4. Losing good prospects before you can hire them

To add more pressure, the average cost of hiring is 16 to 20 percent the position's base salary in direct costs and productivity loss, and the hire rate is only 50 percent.[33]

There's a lot at stake, and your business can suffer if you don't recruit well. After all, you are who you hire.

BREAKING DOWN THE RECRUITING PROCESS

Given how many businesses face problems finding the right people, you're probably well aware of all the challenges we just touched upon. Let's make your job a little easier.

#1: WRITE THE JOB DESCRIPTION

A job description is important and powerful, and it's the first place to start when recruiting.

For starters, a good job description offers several benefits:

- It ensures you know what you're looking for.
- It can be reused for additional hires and as part of a contract.
- It is useful during interviewing and the selection process.

33 Center for American Progress, November 2012.

- It improves your hiring capabilities and trains your team.
- It helps you effectively manage your team members.

Put another way, a solid job description helps with recruiting, selection, interviewing, orientation, training, performance reviews, and establishing compensation.

Let's build one. Write out the following:

- **Position summary.** An overview of the purpose of the role. Keep it around four sentences.
- **Reporting.** To whom does this role report?
- **Soft skills.** Think of personality traits and natural abilities like effective communication, motivation, adaptability, leadership, persuasion, problem-solving, time management, and work ethic.
- **Hard skills.** These are the actual skills and qualifications required to do the job. They include proficiency in a foreign language, degrees and certifications, computer programming, typing speed, and machine operation, among other things.
- **Role expectations.** How many hours per week are required for this position? What other basic requirements need to be met for this role, such as location?
- **Responsibilities.** What duties will the recruit be expected to perform?

- **Salary and benefits.** What is the remuneration for this role? What benefits can a team member expect? How is performance measured? What are the opportunities for growth?
- **Mandatory testing.** This can include drug, aptitude, behavioral, or intelligence tests. It can also include background checks, team member referencing, driving records, and convictions.
- **Establish scoring procedures.** How are you going to score recruits? What elements carry the greatest priority? Write all the hard and soft skills out in order of priority so you know exactly what you're looking for.

Follow this process for every new position that arises. This document should be something kept long-term and potentially used repeatedly, tweaked, and refined as needed.

#2: FIND QUALIFIED CANDIDATES

As mentioned earlier, the best method of referral is from your personal and professional networks. Ask customers for recommendations or ask suppliers who their strongest purchasing agents are. Turn team members into talent spotters and ask them who they think would be a good fit.

Don't just look for talent when you need to recruit. Search for people you want to hire on a constant basis, and then reach out and make contact with them. The bigger your talent pool, the easier it is to recruit.

Here are some things you need to do to find the best candidates:

- Get referrals from personal and professional networks.
- Get referrals from team members, and consider offering a referral bonus.
- Engage friends of your business, again offering a referral bounty.
- Hire recruiters. They can be useful assets, but potentially costly.
- Use an online sourcing system to track and follow up with suitable future candidates.

Getting a stable of talent in place before you need it ensures a ready supply of interested, qualified candidates.

#3: INTERVIEWING AND SELECTION

At some point, you'll need to pull people from your talent pool and interview them for one of your open positions. Whether this is someone you know or someone you've identified, there are multiple steps to the process.

Remember, interviewing isn't one-size-fits-all. Use a series of structured interviews to select the best talent.

Screening

You can skip this step if you know the candidate reasonably well. Phone-based screening should take no more than ten minutes. Five questions should do it:

- What are your career goals?
- What do you excel at professionally?
- What are you not so strong at professionally?
- What do you prefer not to do professionally?
- How would you rate your previous positions and your managers on a scale of one to ten?

If you have time left, you can ask any other relevant questions that might come up. However, it's best to keep things brief. After all, the purpose of this call is to weed out weaker candidates. Keeping things short helps you maintain control of the conversation and screen more effectively.

Script out the conversation in full. As you move through your script, have the job description and scoring factors in front of you and take notes. Be curious, and don't be afraid to go a little off-script. When necessary, use open-ended questions like, "How so?" and "Tell me more" to draw out more information. If at all possible, record the conversation (abiding by any rules or regulations that exist where you operate).

The Webinar

Those who get through the screening process need a more comprehensive interview as soon as possible. I normally ask a candidate to schedule and set up a webinar, because it lets me see who can handle potentially unfamiliar technology without too much guidance and who responds in a timely manner. When you get on the call, what can you see in the background? Is the interviewee set up in a quiet, professional location, or can you see an unmade bed or a busy coffee shop behind them?

I don't ask too many questions in this twenty-minute call. Yes, it's an opportunity to follow up on the information you ascertained in the screening call, but it's also your opportunity to learn how the candidate communicates. Pay attention to both body language and verbal cues. Candidates should come to their interview prepared, so letting them ask questions identifies how much preparation they've put in.

The In-Person Interview

Ideally, multiple interviewers should attend an in-person interview. While one asks questions, the other can listen closely and observe nonverbal communication.

Interviewers must walk a fine line. On one hand, you want to gain as much knowledge as you can. On the other, you must also make sure you don't ask the wrong questions and violate any discriminatory laws.

My solution to this challenge is simple. I only ask the following three questions:

- Why are you specifically qualified for the role as it has been described to you?
- Explain how these qualities and qualifications will provide a positive return on investment for the company, specific to the role for which you are interviewing.
- What personal values do you have that will benefit the company and your colleagues?

I value the third question above the others. Candidates who dodge it immediately disqualify themselves.

These simple, open-ended questions are designed to elicit information from the candidate. Further, as the candidate answers, they will usually provide a great deal of information that you can't legally ask for. If they don't answer fully enough, use the same open-ended prompts like, "Tell me more," or "How so?"

The Social Interview

By now, you're fairly certain who you want to hire. It may even be down to just one candidate. Depending on how many prospective team members you have left in the running, the social interview is crucial, since it establishes how well a person will fit in with your team.

This step is more important than it may seem at first. However, since many businesses have less than seven team members, adding an extra person to that team can cause serious disruption.

The social interview is your chance to bring together as many team members as you can—especially those who will work closely with the potential hire. This can occur over lunch, coffee, or drinks. Invite and brief your team, invite the candidate, and immediately when it's over, solicit feedback from your team. While you have the final say, your team's input is important, and they may have insights that you missed.

#4: THE SALE

You're not truly finished with the interview process until your preferred candidate officially becomes a team member. This means that once you've established which candidates you want, you need to persuade them to join your team.

Think of it this way: you're trying to attract the best talent, so you need to show them you're the best company. Express that you're as concerned with the fit for them as you are for the company. The majority of companies don't do this, so your attention to this detail will set you apart.

Here are five things to consider:

- **Values.** How does your company vision and culture match the interviewee's goals, strengths, and values?
- **Family.** How can your company make the transition as easy as possible for the candidate's family?
- **Freedom.** The best team members loathe being micromanaged, so express it clearly that team members have the autonomy to make decisions within your company.
- **Remuneration.** Make it clear that team members are paid on a tight schedule and that your company is economically stable. Tell interviewees how their performance is reviewed, detail your perks and bonuses,

and describe ways in which they can increase their own remuneration.

- **Fun.** Interpersonal relationships and a happy work environment are vital, so make sure the business's ideals, opportunities for fun, and team culture are clearly expressed to the candidate.

It's incredibly disheartening to offer a candidate a job only to have them turn you down. Selling your company using these five elements ensures that a candidate's decision isn't purely a financial one.

#5: ONBOARDING

I vividly remember turning up for my first day at a big tech company and being asked to wait in the lobby until someone was ready to see me—which took *three hours*. Nobody wants to be that type of employer. The following are four suggestions on how to be the best new boss.

Get Ready

Make sure you're prepared for your new recruit before they arrive. Get them set up in your system, with all the login credentials, passwords, and email addresses they'll need. Provide a training process along with an HR manual, and have their desk ready for them. Because you'll have to repeat the process for every person you hire, create a checklist and stick to it.

I've heard business people say, "Let's see if the new hire works out before we buy their business cards or spend any money on them." That's the wrong attitude. You want your new recruit to feel welcomed and wanted, which in turn will make them feel better about taking the job and more inclined to work harder.

A little extra effort will go a long way. Besides, printing a stack of business cards doesn't cost much when compared to the cost of hiring another new team member.

First Impressions

Make the right impression on the first day by having something delivered to a new team member's home address. Send flowers, cookies, or some other small token to the recruit's family. Attach a note saying something like, "Thank you for your support. We can't wait to work with so-and-so." This way, at the end of the first day, both the recruit and their family will react positively to your company.

A common present we give to the families of new team members is a money plant—also commonly referred to as a jade tree. We had someone retire a few years ago who had been with us for about five years. On his last day, he sent us a picture of the money plant we'd given him on his first day. It was still thriving, and he and his family had enjoyed living with it all those years.

Build a Relationship

Part of successful onboarding is ensuring the recruit's immediate circle feels good about where their friend or family member has started to work. Close friends and family will ask a recruit how their new job is for the first few months. Since these people are vitally important to your recruit and influence that person's thoughts and behavior, you want them to feel confident about you as an employer.

Why does this matter so much? Well, people rarely leave a job in complete isolation. They talk it over with family and friends first. If this support network suggests the recruit can get a better job elsewhere, there's a good chance they'll leave. This is definitely not what you want. Include ongoing communication and participation in social events for your recruit's immediate family.

The Welcome Party

Many companies throw leaving parties. It's standard practice and it seems like a nice thing to do, but is there much
point in spending money on a team member who won't
be coming back? Perhaps, if you know they'll refer other
candidates down the road.

However, I strongly suggest you throw a welcome party
instead. This lets old hands and new hires meet in an
informal setting and makes everyone feel valued and
welcome. So bring in lunch, promote a happy hour, or
open up an online hangout. Make their new workplace
feel like *home*.

WHY YOU SHOULD HIRE SLOWLY

We started the chapter with the quote, "Slow to hire, quick to fire." I live by this motto when hiring at my own companies. Here are several reasons why I do this.

1. Hiring fast can result in a costly mistake. Don't rush to fill an open position because you feel pressured by the idea your company needs to grow rapidly. Take your time and hire the right person.

2. Take your time with the interview process and don't skip the social step. This ensures the team member shares your company's values and fits in well with the rest of the team.

3. By taking time before you hire, you may find that other team members can take on the extra work or that it isn't as much as you anticipated. You may be able to save hiring costs and keep the work within your existing team.

4. You can be certain of making the right offer if you don't rush into it. Getting to know your candidate lets you see what motivates them aside from salary so you can make an attractive, personalized offer.

The moment you believe a person is no longer a good fit, you are right. Fire them now. This matters for a few reasons. First, if you procrastinate over firing, others will question why you're avoiding making a tough decision. Second, a bad apple will poison the whole team. Their negativity will infect others. Third, your clients and stakeholders will be disappointed if you're hanging on to someone who really isn't a good fit for your first-class team.

As the old saying goes, "Your team is only as strong as your weakest link." Don't let your weak links pull down your entire team.

FOREVER WHERE I WANT TO BE

I loved living in Dubai, but it was a comparatively small city then, and being there for too long wasn't great for morale. Remember, you should always be exactly where you want to be, and Dubai is a fantastic hub for international travel. In the dozen years I lived there, I never stayed in Dubai for more than three months at a time. In fact, I usually traveled at least once a month.

One such trip involved attending an entrepreneur's conference in LA with an evening event at the Playboy Mansion. As expected, the party was high-end with appetizers, music, and mingling both inside and outside the grotto. I was at the bar beside a few A-list actors waiting to get a round of drinks when a beautiful woman in a cocktail dress asked me to pass her a drink.

As I complied, I looked for her conference nametag. She asked me what I was doing, and I explained that I was looking to see her name. She told me it was Miss July 1998, or Summer for short.

As we got to talking, I immediately knew I wanted her on my team. I admired her ingenuity, her ambition, her knowledge of what she wanted and where she wanted to be, and her plan to get there. Her charisma was unmistakable. Here was a woman who could make things happen.

How do you get the best person to join your team? You sell it. My favorite method is finding out what motivates the person you're selling to. As luck had it, a friend was getting married a few weeks later in New York, so I called them and asked if I could bring a girl I met at the Playboy Mansion as my plus-one. That was the easy sell.

However, persuading a Californian girl to fly to New York on the anniversary of 9/11—and with someone she'd only just met who lived in Dubai—meant I had to sell like I'd never sold before.

After learning that she dreamed of visiting every Major League Baseball stadium, I checked to see if the Yankees were playing. They were. I'd found my golden ticket. To make a long story short, we'll just say that was quite a date.

That's how I persuaded the one person I really wanted to be on my team and who eventually became my wife. It was a tough sell, probably the single most important sale of my life, but ever since, I've been exactly where I wanted to be—by her side.

THE PASSION, PROFITABILITY, AND HAPPINESS INDEX

Up to now, I've been giving you a series of bullet points to explain everything. This time, we'll keep it simple. The single thing that makes me profitable, lets me live my passion, and brings me happiness is the ability to live my life with the person I choose to be with.

THREE KEY TAKEAWAYS

Team building may feel like a great mystery, but with a good process and a commitment to doing things the right way instead of doing them quickly, you can dramatically increase your chances of making the right decision.

Here are the three most important takeaways:

- Recruiting is a continuum. Always be looking for great recruits.
- Systemize your recruitment so it improves over time.
- Selling is a vital part of recruitment.

Now that you know how to build a team member who is exactly where they want to be, let's talk about how to nurture those relationships and maximize your return.

NOW FOR SOME FUN

What is your favorite question to ask during a recruiting interview?

Once you've given it some thought, share here:

http://exactlywhereyouwanttobe.com/hiring

CHAPTER 10

NURTURING YOUR TEAM

———

Good leadership consists of showing average people how to do the work of superior people.

—JOHN D. ROCKEFELLER

Meet Steve of the nutritional ingredients company, RIBUS.[34] In operation since 1992, RIBUS supplies natural and organic rice ingredients to global food, beverage, supplement, and pet companies.

As Steve will tell you, it wasn't easy cracking this market, which has traditionally relied on synthetic ingredients to cut costs. However, Steve's solution was twofold. First, he developed and patented a proprietary technology that

---
[34] www.ribus.com

could produce natural products for this market. Then, he began lobbying at the federal level to influence legislation so that certain industries had to use his patented natural ingredients over synthetic ones.

This is a remarkable business model that is poised for exponential growth after over a decade of development. When I first met Steve, I saw a man who was the epitome of planning and perseverance. However, while he was strong in certain aspects of his business, outsourcing to over a hundred independent sales agents, he couldn't figure out why his core team wasn't performing as well as he desired.

The more I learned, the more I could see a clear deviation between what Steve thought his team's responsibilities were and what they thought. With the problem identified, we put on a half-day workshop that brought everybody to the same page and laid out what his team needed to do to create more success. In the process, Steve developed a better understanding of who his long-term players were and where he'd need to invest future resources. Even more, he came away far better equipped to lead his team.

TEAMWORK: THE SECRET SAUCE OF SUCCESS

Do you ever get the feeling that someone doesn't have the same view as you? Does your team feel like it's pulling in different directions? Do you wish you had more present-day resources for future growth?

Many businesses I work with want to clearly define their teams' roles and responsibilities. And why not? Better communication always leads to a more comfortable working environment, more effective leadership, and a sense of common purpose.

TATTOOS FOR THE TEAM

Steve has come a long way, but he's still not quite at the level of Jason Quinn's hugely successful restaurant, Playground DTSA. You may remember this story from Chapter 1, but if not, here's a recap. Before embarking on his 2011 *Great Food Truck Race*, Jason dreamed of taking his truck and expanding it into a restaurant like no other. He succeeded, and his culinary empire continues to grow.

It's not only that Jason sells great food coupled with a winning business model. He's also created a culture where some people love their jobs so much, they get matching brand tattoos. Just imagine your team members doing the same thing!

CLEAR ROLES MATTER

Teamwork improves when individual members understand their roles and the roles of others. This allows them to focus and perform independently. Teams without this kind of clarity often waste energy negotiating roles and playing politics.

Here's one way to look at it: although *you're* entrepreneurial, the majority of people aren't. In fact, most people like clear parameters and focused direction. Your business depends on your team knowing exactly where they should be and what they should be doing.

DEFINING ROLES AND RESPONSIBILITIES

Now that we understand the value of clearly defined roles, how do we go about defining them? What's the recipe for success?

With a good process, it's not that tough. In fact, you can approach it in a variety of ways—meeting one-on-one with every team member, working alongside your business coach, or by designing a group exercise.

WHICH IS WHICH?

First, it's important we're all on the same page with our terminology, since roles and responsibilities are not the same thing. It's up to you to know which is which—or, if you're running a costume store, which witch is which, as it were.

Think of a role as a designation, or where a person falls within the business—such as sales, marketing, strategic management, customer service, technical support, and so on. From there, each role comes with a set of responsibilities that the team member must perform to fulfill that role.

In other words, the role is the general term, and the responsibilities are the specifics. Depending on your business, it's possible for more than one person to have the same role.

DEFINING ROLES

With that out of the way, let's start defining the different roles within your own business:

1. List every member of your team.
2. For each one, designate a role—the general area of the business for which they are responsible.

3. List the key responsibilities of each role. What are the specific tasks and duties? Ask your team for their thoughts and understanding of their duties. Remember to include the obligations for which they are held accountable within their roles.

4. Attribute time to each responsibility. It's often easier to attribute a percentage of a day or week. Average it out if the work is cyclical over a week, month, quarter, or year.

5. Once you've got your list, with the assistance and insights of your team, review it fully for accuracy.

6. Once you've reached a consensus with your team, ask them each to rank, in order, their perception of responsibility in terms of bringing value to the business within their own role. Then ask them to rate their desire to complete each responsibility from +10 (love it) to -10 (don't love it).

This last step lets you see whether you've got the right people in the right roles. While everyone will have tasks they dislike, if you see someone has too many negatives, they may be in the wrong role and therefore not as effective.

QUESTION TIME

Ask each team member how their role would differ, and where they'd fit in it if the business was three times larger than it currently is. The response is usually:

- Two more people doing the same role
- Breaking the role down in some way, such as senior and junior positions

This is a good basic framework, but here are a few other key questions to ask your team:

- How would the team within your role expand?
- Would you use permanent, temporary, or independent people?
- Would you outsource some elements?
- Where would these people be located?
- What would you need to make this happen?

Asking questions like these can lead to important insights, helping you to see the inner workings of your business in an entirely new way.

PROGRAMMING SUCCESS

Defining your team's roles and responsibilities gives everyone a clear set of expectations to which they should aspire.

But the work doesn't stop there. By measuring your team's progress, you can learn a great deal about your team's strengths and weaknesses and adjust accordingly.

KPIS

Key performance indicators (KPIs) are vital measurements for tracking the responsibilities and successes of your team. If you're measuring the right things, you can use this data to help drive your business forward. The cliché is true: what gets measured gets managed.

Establish and track a small number of metrics that are crucial to the function of each role. These KPIs can be as broad as "deliver market-leading consulting services" or as narrow as "make sure we send out invoices and collect payments in a timely manner." Whatever the case, be sure to strike a balance. Too few and the dataset will be incomplete and of little value. Too many and it becomes laborious for your team and nullifies the whole process.

Here's a critical question that helps team members better manage themselves: "How would you, as manager of this role, evaluate the team?" Because they are intimately acquainted with their roles and responsibilities, they can define at least the basis of three key performance indicators for evaluation purposes.

Some may struggle the first time they attempt this, but it'll get easier, eventually taking no more than fifteen minutes. Some, however, will need a little more encouragement. Give these team members a copy of their job description, past performance reviews, the company goals and objectives, their own definition of their role and responsibilities, and sales call transcripts or important emails.

MAKE IT SMART

The KPIs your team came up with may be great, but now you need to make them real. How, exactly, are you going to measure success? Each KPI needs to fulfill one or more SMART goals:

- **Specific.** What exactly are we measuring? Target a specific area for improvement.
- **Measurable.** How will you check progress? Quantify or establish an indicator of progress.
- **Attainable.** Is it realistic? What do they need to make it possible?
- **Relevant.** Why are they doing it? Does it matter to the individual and company? What results are achievable with the available resources?
- **Time-based.** When will it be completed?

SMART goals keep you on track, breaking down a specific goal into more actionable components. The more you can remove the guesswork, the more successful your team will be.

SMART IN ACTION

How do SMART goals work? Say that our KPI is "invoicing and collecting payments in a timely manner." To achieve this, we need at least two SMART goals—one for invoicing and one for collecting payments. Focusing on invoicing, your SMART goal could look something like this:

- **Specific.** We're talking about invoices being processed and sent to the correct customer contact.
- **Measurable.** Send out within twenty-four hours of fulfillment in 98 percent of cases per week.
- **Attainable.** Brenda is currently achieving a 70 percent success rate, so 98 percent seems attainable. It would help to update the accounting software to the latest version.
- **Relevant.** Debtors pay faster if they receive the invoice closer to the fulfillment date.
- **Time-based.** Achieve this measurable goal by the end of the quarter.

Using the SMART system, if you can measure your goal and define a timeline, you've got a solid KPI.

SMART GOAL APPROVAL

Once your team has completed their SMART goals to represent their KPIs, you or your team's direct manager needs to approve them. Look for three things:

1. Do the KPIs properly address the priorities of the role?
2. Are the KPIs meaningful to the business?
3. Are they SMART?

What does "meaningful for the business" really mean? Clarity is important here, so let's look at an example.

Say that your office support person makes a KPI about keeping the office looking clean and professional, with fresh flowers put out every week. While this is important, it's not that essential or meaningful to the success of your business. In this instance, the person would need to define a more appropriate KPI. Not every responsibility needs a KPI, only those that lead to measurable success for your business.

GET ON WITH IT

Once you've approved the KPIs, it's time for your team to get on with their jobs. As a great leader, you'll need to check in with your team members on a regular basis to see how they are progressing with their SMART goals. If they're doing well, congratulate them and offer encouragement. If they are struggling, ask if there's anything you can do to make the SMART goals more achievable:

- Do they need to modify any behaviors?
- Do priorities need to be amended?
- Are new or updated processes needed?
- Are new tools required?
- Are additional resources necessary?
- Does the SMART goal need updating?

Business moves quickly, so what was initially a quarterly goal may not be appropriate for the whole quarter. Nothing wrong with that, but now you can address these issues objectively because you have data.

REACHING THE END OF THE SMART GOAL

Once the timeframe established for a team member's SMART goals has passed, it's time for them to report back with the results. As long as your goal was realistic and achievable, there are three basic scenarios:

1. **Goal met.** The team member is good at their role, and everyone is happy.
2. **Goal not met.** Nothing unforeseen occurred, but the team member fell short.
3. **Goal not met.** Something unforeseen occurred, so priorities changed.

In any of these scenarios, sit down with the team member to discuss where improvements could be made. If the team member delivered, perhaps you could set a more ambitious SMART goal. If the team member did not, find out why and if there is anything you can do to better support their efforts.

Either way, after every report, ask your team members to set new KPIs for the upcoming work weeks, months, or quarters. Some will be repeated, while others will be new. It depends on your business and each person's role.

At my businesses, we love KPIs and SMART goals because they are simple, relevant to every business, and appropriate for team members at any level. Most importantly, they work, and they keep your team happy and focused.

ANNUAL REVIEWS

What is the value of the annual review? You don't like doing them, and your team doesn't like being subjected to them. You get stressed at having to bring up the topic and arrange a meeting. Your team members get stressed preparing for it.

Nobody likes the annual review because nobody likes being in that kind of situation. I've had team members get so stressed over annual reviews that they've started crying before the review even began.

To be blunt, the reviews themselves are pretty dumb too. Can you actually remember everything that happened at work over the last year? How do you objectively review that? How can you give constructive feedback, help your team member improve, and work to motivate them? Even if by some miracle you both agree on something that happened eleven months ago, there's no way both parties will leave that meeting happy.

SHOW ME THE MONEY

Imagine you're a staff member sitting through your annual review. All you really want to know, regardless of how well the review is going, is how much of a raise you're going to get. How much more money will be in your paycheck?

This is a difficult conversation, which is why so many leaders skip this part of the review and just give out blanket raises each year.

When you do this, however, you kill team member mobility, and your talent pool stagnates. In five or ten years, you and your team member aren't happy. First off, they're overpaid by this point, so you've probably come to resent both them and the situation their salary has put you in. Worse, your team members are stuck in a job with no room for mobility, because other companies are only paying the going rate, and they don't want to take a pay cut to move on. This is exactly where you don't want to be—a business with more overhead than it needs and no team member mobility.

THE OATH

Before I let you in on the secret to avoid this situation, you need to take the following oath:

> As a responsible business owner, I commit not to share this secret with any non-business owner, and under no circumstances will I share it with a team member of any organization.

Never, under any circumstances, should you be holding an annual review for a team member. They are unfair and subjective, leading to an unhappy team and unnecessary business costs. Instead, here are four things you should be doing:

1. Promote a culture where team members can raise issues and concerns with you at any time, not just once a year.
2. Measure your team's work through objective KPIs.
3. Reward team members based on objective KPIs.
4. Hold annual career development meetings.

The goal here is to be a more dynamic and compassionate business leader while still protecting your company's own best interests. The more you give regular, balanced feedback, the more you will get in return, and the better your business will run.

THE VALUE OF CAREER DEVELOPMENT MEETINGS

Think of career development meetings as the opposite of the performance review. Instead of reviewing a team member's past performance, you work *with* them to build their own skills and value within the company.

In these development meetings, discuss any available opportunities for advancement, as well as the necessary resources, training, and support your team member needs to get there. This type of meeting is more nurturing, positive, and motivating, and results in a happy, engaged team with better longevity.

THE BIG PICTURE

When it comes down to it, the success of your company is dependent upon the success of your team, which needs three things to thrive:

1. A system to follow that includes all the tools and resources to do the job
2. Accountability from the supervisor
3. The motivation to keep going

Annual reviews actually defeat this goal, but an organization committed to career development and a culture of regular feedback is far more likely to succeed in the long run.

MOTIVATION

Here's one last takeaway as we approach the end of the chapter. Many business leaders worry about how to keep their teams motivated. It can be a tough road to navigate, but as the owner, motivating your team is absolutely part of your job description. Need a little help in this area? Here are eight tips to help you boost team member morale.

SET EXPECTATIONS

Your team loves to know what's expected of them. Using KPIs and SMART goals helps to give your team members clear objectives.

HAVE A DAILY HUDDLE

Open communication is crucial. How much communication is going on in your office right now—verbally or online? A fast five-minute standing huddle at the start of every day keeps communication open and everybody on the same page. Moreover, they help motivate and energize your team.

If you're not all in one location, do a virtual huddle; there are plenty of tools to help with this. And remember, you're the business owner, so it's crucial that wherever you are or whatever else you're doing, you never miss one of these team huddles.

SURPRISE THE SCHEDULE

You're the boss, so motivate your team with a surprise in the schedule. If there's been a long weekend, let your team start late the first day back. Or maybe it's the start of the beach season, so let the team finish early on Friday. Maybe motivation is flagging on hump day, so treat your team to an early finish and a drink. Or perhaps the clocks just changed; how about letting your team arrive an hour late the following business day?[35]

WHY ARE YOU IN BUSINESS?

Your team needs to know why you're in business, aside from making money. Every owner I've ever met starts their business for the good of something else, for the passion, or for the challenge. Share your start-up story, your core values, or your guiding principles.

SAY THANK YOU

Say it often, be genuine, and smile while you say it. People like to be appreciated, so start showing your thanks.

---

35 Perhaps this level of niceness doesn't fit with your management style. That's okay; we're all different. However, it's not just about being nice. Research shows that a well-motivated, happy team is more efficient and effective. You may even be saving lives. A 2015 study by CU Boulder discovered a 17 percent increase in traffic fatalities on the Monday after we put our clocks forward.

LISTEN

Let your team vent if they need to. Like all of us, sometimes team members have things they need to get off their chest. Not every comment needs to be acted upon. Mostly, it's just venting, and team members often just need to talk things out.

FRAME THE ENVIRONMENT

How do you want your team members to act and feel when they're at work? And what can you do to their environment to promote it? A study by the Department for Business Innovation and Skills in the UK found that a team's well-being is strongly correlated to team productivity and performance. Perhaps one of the largest factors of well-being is the physical workplace. Team members who enjoy and like the environment they are part of will be more engaged, productive, happy, and healthy. There are numerous reports and studies, such as Gellner's Workplace Index and The Leesman Index, that explore the relationship between the working environment and business performance.

REWARD YOUR TEAM

Show your appreciation, bring smiles, and boost motivation with unexpected rewards. This doesn't have to be costly; it can be as simple as sending a handwritten thank you note for a job well done or rewarding your best team member with flexible hours. Offer a premium parking spot, throw a pizza party, buy lunch, give an extra day's paid leave, hold casual Fridays, give a rental car for a week, or start a wall of fame. Alternatively, bring in a car detailing service, have a masseuse visit the office, buy lunch, or offer to pay for an educational course for your team members. Give away movie tickets or support family interests. Have a "Bring your dog to work" day, or make your office dog-friendly.

THE BIG PICTURE ON MOTIVATION

As a great leader, you not only want to motivate your team members to be the best they can be, but you also want to keep them around. These two basic needs go hand-in-hand. A happy, motivated team sticks around, so start thinking about what changes you can make today. As an added bonus, word will soon spread about your great, motivational culture, and you'll attract more high-caliber talent.

If you get to know your team, you'll be able to provide the most relevant perks. For example, a client of mine needed to boost motivation during the busy tax season at his accounting company. We came up with an array of fantastic ideas, including many from the previous sections.

However, do you want to know the most well-received gift? New calculators for the whole team. Yes, sometimes the simple things can speak volumes, if they're relevant.

FORGED IN FLAMES

My business in Dubai continued to grow and excel, leading to bigger and better brands as clients. Soon, we secured a lucrative contract for a well-known theme park and were arranging a press conference for the brand. This involved renting a large room and inviting a host of journalists to report on the big announcement.

As you can appreciate, there's a huge amount of preparation involved in creating an event of this nature. In fact, it took our entire team to pull it off. Due to the cultural environment in Dubai, this team was exceptionally diverse, with small groups all speaking different languages, hailing from different countries, and representing different backgrounds. However, because we all knew our tasks, responsibilities, and common goals, we were all able to move in the same direction to get the job done.

The night before the big press conference, we were fully prepared. The venue was set up, the journalists were invited, and the client was briefed. The following morning, I was on my way to the office early, where I'd arranged to meet some of the team to pick up press kits and materials to take to the press conference.

As I drew closer, I saw a thick plume of smoke coming from the office building and a number of fire trucks in the vicinity. Naturally, I grew a little concerned.

The firefighters at the entrance didn't want anyone entering the building, but I had a job to do—and a major client depending on my company. Without thinking, I ran up the three stories to our smoke-filled office, picked up as many press kits as I could, dropped them off at my car, and raced back in for another go. After about three trips, a couple of my team members arrived and joined me in my effort, furiously racing in and out of the burning building.

Now how's that for a team-building exercise?

THE PASSION, PROFITABILITY, AND HAPPINESS INDEX

Was I exactly where I wanted to be? Absolutely. The fact that there was smoke building up in our office wasn't really an issue. We were contracted to hold the year's biggest press conference in the country, we'd done so much preparation, and my team and I were doing whatever was necessary—including running into a burning building—to fulfill our obligation:

- **Passion.** We were passionate about delivering the best service, so much so that we'd run into a burning building to pull it off.
- **Profitability.** This was the country's largest press conference of the year and a huge client for us. Profitability follows when you deliver for a great customer.
- **Happiness.** To this day, it's hard to describe the pride I had in my team as I watched them run into a burning building for our company.

You'd never ask a team member to run into a burning building for you, but when the whole team is motivated and you're pulling in the same direction, people want to do whatever it takes.

THE TAKEAWAYS

How's that for some helpful team-building lessons? Remember, you don't need to build a team willing to run into a burning building to succeed, but if you can foster a culture where everyone firmly believes they're in it together, you'll be surprised at the lengths to which your team members will go.

Here are my three big takeaways:

1. Make your culture so alluring that your team wants to tattoo it on themselves or run into a burning building.
2. Set KPIs and SMART goals every quarter.
3. No annual reviews. Ever.

With a good team comes exceptional growth. And when this happens, it's time to start focusing on the big picture rather than the day-to-day tasks of your business. Read on to the next chapter to find out more.

NOW FOR SOME FUN

What is your favorite way to motivate your team?

Once you've given it some thought, share here:

http://exactlywhereyouwanttobe.com/team

CHAPTER 11

GETTING OUT OF THE WEEDS

We are what we repeatedly do. Excellence,
then, is not an act, but a habit.

—ARISTOTLE

Meet Ed Simons of Simons Accountancy Corporation,
an award-winning accounting firm that specializes in
helping clients minimize or defer taxes.[36] Ed also offers
traditional compliance in the areas of individual partnerships, corporate work, and fiduciary. Ed is exceptionally
talented in these areas, and you won't find anyone more
detail-oriented and trustworthy. Like a good leader, Ed
credits much of his success to his outstanding team.

---

36 www.simonscorp.com

When we first started working together, one of his challenges was that he simply couldn't take on any more clients because, when tax season arrived, he'd routinely work over a hundred hours a week. Understandably, he felt he owed it to both his family and his team to stop increasing his personal workload.

I'm sure you've experienced something similar. You know when you're working too hard, those around you suffer. Nevertheless, you're driven to continue and increase your success. However, as I told Ed, at a certain point the only way to improve your business is to take a step back and let others help shoulder the load.

The first step to improving your situation is to get a better understanding of your own process and workflow. With this in mind, Ed wrote out his average workflow, identified areas for refinement, optimized the process, and committed to following it.

However, Ed knew it wasn't enough for him alone to follow this new process. So, he rolled it out to his team and found it improved customer service, reduced work hours, and changed everyone's vision for the following tax season. The team was happier, Ed worked less, and the company became more effective and profitable. Since this change,

Ed has been able to expand his business and get closer to being exactly where he wants to be.

If you run a small or medium business, you've probably felt like Ed from time to time. It's easy to get caught up in all the day-to-day tasks that make your business special. However, looking back at your personal vision, is that really where you want to be? Should you still be performing so many different duties yourself, or should you shift your focus and start working *on* the business rather than *in* the business?

THE BUSINESS PROCESS EXPLAINED

The term "business process" was conceived by Aaron Smith in 1776 and has given rise to areas of study such as operations development, operations management, and a variety of business management systems. These systems have in turn paved the way for business process management (BPM) software, which helps companies to automate process management.

At its simplest, a business process requires a series of specific actions designed to achieve an objective. Most BPM software operates continuously, though it still allows for ad hoc actions. The number of steps and systems dictates whether a process is simple or complex, short-term or long-term.

It might seem obvious to think that businesses must have processes in place, but many don't—even some large ones. Remember, processes ultimately help you find more happiness and time for the things that matter. The only way to build something that has the potential to grow bigger than you is by using teams, automation, and delegation.

WHAT ARE PROCESS FLOW DIAGRAMS?

A process flow diagram, or a business process diagram, is a road map for the implementation of defined processes. It outlines the expected outcomes and provides a solid foundation from which to build.

Here are the benefits to diagramming a business process:

1. It lets you look at the big picture and account for all scenarios.
2. It helps you fully understand your process so you can identify areas for optimization.
3. It provides a visual aid everyone can adhere to, ensuring everyone is on the same page. This promotes a consistent service level.

4. It helps to prevent up-front errors and prevent unnecessary changes.

There's a good chance you've read Michael Gerber's *E-Myth*, one of the most popular books in its genre, which describes how processes are the key to working on your business foundation. However, if you're like a lot of business leaders, while you may understand the *need* for business processes, you still struggle to implement them in your own business.

Business process diagrams are standard essential operating documents that streamline your workflow and increase profitability. Before we get into the specifics of producing a process for creating processes, we need to establish the difference between a process and a task list. A process often encompasses multiple people—including clients—with the required actions ordered sequentially. A task list, on the other hand, is more granular, usually unordered, and is for the attention of only one person.

THE PROCESS FOR CREATING A PROCESS

As with so many of the concepts outlined in this book, crafting a good business process requires a good process in itself.

DEVELOP A PROCESS ENTRY

Creating a list of all of your processes may seem simplistic, but it's necessary. Even if you think you already know all your processes, using a list as a visual prompt helps you think about process prioritization. Which processes do you already have that are optimized, and which ones are yet to be implemented or are in desperate need of retooling?

KNOW YOUR OBJECTIVE

Clarify what you're trying to do by listing your goals. For example, at the top level, that could be "getting out of the weeds"—which, not coincidentally, is the name of this chapter. Beyond that, you may want to increase efficiency, improve customer service, achieve a quicker turnaround, reduce costs, or outsource more efficiently. From there, you can identify the processes you need to prioritize to achieve those goals.

THREE-STEP DIAGRAMMING PROCESS

Keeping it short and simple, your diagramming process should follow this pattern:

1. Draw up an initial diagram based on your own knowledge.
2. Gather additional inputs from others in your company.

3. Incorporate these requirements into the diagram.

You may need to repeat steps two and three several times to ensure everyone is satisfied with the result.

The Initial Diagram

Create an initial diagram that offers a general overview of what you think the process should look like. You can always ask a manager or your business coach to help you. However, don't ask for the input of the person actually doing the process. Next, create a flowchart of the process that includes every activity, listed in order, linked sequentially from one to the next:

1. Begin with the opening event in the process and draw a circle around it. For example, this could be an email order from a client.
2. Draw a line to another box and fill that box with the first action required to begin the process workflow. In our example, that could be "Add work order to internal delivery system." Continue through the process in this manner.
3. When you reach a step that requires a decision, draw a diamond around the question, followed by two lines leading from the diamond. The "yes" branch runs horizontally, and the negative or alternative branch

runs vertically. For our example, the question could be, "Is order value under $10K?" If yes, proceed to the next step, if no, create another task offshoot: "Check with accounts for appropriate credit history."

4. Link each activity sequentially and account for actions that run simultaneously.
5. Draw a circle around the final activity of a process to indicate you've reached the process conclusion.

Flowcharts are beneficial in two essential ways. First, they help you visualize your process—perhaps for the first time. Second, the very act of creating the flowchart engages you in your own process, encouraging you to consider the value of every single step.

Gather Additional Requirements

Now is the point at which you consult with the people actually performing the tasks. If you do so beforehand, you risk overwhelming your team member, so make sure you've got a rough process in place with your initial diagram. This way, your team member will be confident and accurate in their feedback—and to be certain, you *will* get feedback.

Before you solicit feedback, take a deep breath. Remind yourself that your team members are intimately acquainted with their roles. They know their jobs better than you do, so be open to whatever they have to say. For instance, your team members could tell you that you've left out a crucial step, that you've included redundant or unnecessary steps, or even that you've created a process that's counterintuitive to their needs.

Revising

After you've received feedback, consider the cause and effect of each action, how they relate to one another, and how they move you closer to your stated objective:

- Each action should be interdependent to achieve the desired outcome.
- Activities may be sequential or parallel; one activity cannot occur before the preceding ones are complete, or two actions may occur simultaneously.

Once you've got your diagram filled out and you and your team are in agreement, it's time to maximize efficiency.

FINALIZING

Up to this point of diagramming, the purpose has been to document the "as-is" process, so it's okay if you have redundant or unnecessary steps. However, now it's time to ensure every single step is justified:

1. Streamline the process and avoid having too many steps to avoid confusion.

2. If you omit actions that are important to your overall business or that are better used toward another objective, take note of them and use them elsewhere.

3. Where you have multiple people working in or completing the same role, it's usually good to choose just one person to work with on the process documentation. Choose based on performance, accuracy, and/ or seniority.

4. Integrate your team member's activity list with your initial process diagram.

5. Once you and the team member are in agreement on all the proper steps, it's time to see where you can increase efficiency, enhance quality, and reduce cost. Consider whether you can reorder some steps, get rid of some altogether, or install any new actions. Are there any parts of the process that can be automated? Share the document with someone you trust and ask for feedback.

6. Look at the document through the eyes of the customer and further consider any improvements you could make. Is the process clear and informative? Is the customer experience prioritized throughout? Is the flow neat, accurate, and user-friendly enough that anyone can pick it up and follow it?

7. Make your changes, then go back to your consulting team member and ask if they agree with your improved process.

Congratulations! You've successfully optimized your business process.

IMPLEMENTING NEW FLOWS

For successful implementation of your new business processes, your manager or other senior team member needs to approve it. You then need to roll it out internally at the team level, which may be as simple as delivering copies of the diagrams, but may also require new tools, automation processes, or training.

If any outside partners, freelancers, or vendors are impacted, they also need to be brought up to speed. Any new partnerships should be established at this time. Make sure everyone is on the same page and that people don't fall back to the old way of working.

SEVEN TIPS FOR GOOD
WORKING PROCESSES

The process of building processes is, well, a process. Here are seven more tips to help things go smoothly.

1. Add screenshots and pictures to the process documents so team members find it easier to implement the changes.

2. Use simple language; simplicity and clarity make it easier to absorb the information and execute the instruction.

3. Most people will start executing a process before they read the whole document, so front-load any need-to-know information—such as any upcoming steps that require precise timing or accuracy.

4. Eradicate vagueness by giving a clear timeline and quality parameters; you'll likely need to refine your processes repeatedly to accomplish this.

5. Explain both the why and the how of a process. Briefly providing your reasoning for a step makes the associated actions clearer. Similarly, an explanation of why you take a specific action makes it easy to spot obsolete actions and processes.

6. Give an example of a completed action or entire process using screenshots to assist in execution.

7. Anticipate problems and include troubleshooting notes for common issues and errors.

Remember, all these tips are meant to guide you and help you avoid common pitfalls in process diagramming. At the end of the day, make sure your process-making approach fits your business needs, and don't be afraid of modifying your approach as needed.

MOSCOW NIGHTS

While living and working in the Middle East, I went to Moscow with twenty-five of my closest friends and their partners—all of whom were business owners like me. Our large group spent a fabulous three-day weekend investigating everything Moscow had to offer, and we weren't disappointed.

One very early morning, we were leaving a club and needed a taxi, which involved a somewhat different process than in other parts of the world. In Moscow, hiring a cab means sticking out your hand and waiting for someone—usually a resident—to stop and give you a ride if they're going in the same direction. Then, you offer them a few dollars for their troubles. In a sense it's like an informal, unregulated version of Uber.

Eventually, we got two cars to stop. Some of us piled into one car, while I and two others got into a dubious-looking Lada, a small, infamously unreliable Russian-made vehicle. Off we went, weaving down wide Soviet-era boulevards and cobblestone streets in a highly suspect car at two in the morning.

Suddenly, a brand new Audi rounded a corner and cut us off, forcing us into the opposite lane and into oncoming traffic. As cars sped past us on either side, I noticed the Audi was mocking us from the other lane and refusing to let us back over. I began to suspect this might be the end for me and my compatriots.

Just when all seemed lost, I saw blue flashing lights come on, and I heard a police siren begin its familiar wail. Perhaps we might actually get out of this crazy situation after all, I thought.

The Audi quickly disappeared down a side street, and as our car pulled back into the right lane, our driver reached down and cut off the lights and siren. He drove on for a few more blocks, got us to our destination, and casually said, "Thanks very much. It's been fun having you in the car. That's two bucks, please."

Once we collected ourselves, we realized what had happened. Unknown to us, our driver was a policeman in an unmarked car who had picked us up while on duty to make a few extra bucks.

THE PASSION, PROFITABILITY, AND HAPPINESS INDEX

Some processes are universal—everybody understands what flashing blue lights and sirens mean—but others can be unique to a business or a place, just like cabbing around in Moscow. Nevertheless, the wild night certainly scored high on my passion, profitability, and happiness index:

- **Passion.** We were exactly where we wanted to be, living it up in Moscow with the chance at some once-in-a-lifetime experiences.
- **Profit.** It's natural for people to bond after such a wild experience. I've done a lot of great business with that group of people since our Moscow trip.
- **Happiness.** Yes, it was a crazy situation, but we were having fun, we trusted the ride-sharing system, went with the process, and ultimately arrived safely at our hotel.

Here's the moral of the story. Some systems may seem bizarre to us, but if there is a process in place, it may not be perfect, but it will most likely get the job done.

THREE TAKEAWAYS

What do you do, how do you do it, and can you repeat it? The businesses that can answer these questions tend to stick around. Here are the biggest lessons from this chapter:

1. Take your business to the next level by working *on* the business, not *in* the business.
2. Business processes allow for automation and delegation.
3. Your processes are a powerful success factor.

Now that you're armed with a solid foundation of process-minded thinking, it's time to get to work. If you can commit to crafting reliable processes for every aspect of your business, you'll have a leg up on a lot of your competitors.

What processes do you have written down for your business that you would be willing to share with other business owners?

Once you've given it some thought, share here:

http://exactlywhereyouwanttobe.com/processes

CHAPTER 12

ADVANCED DREAM FULFILLMENT

———

I feel that luck is preparation meeting opportunity.

—OPRAH WINFREY

Meet Gary Arch, the third-generation family owner of BMR Insurance.[37] Proudly serving Orange County for over seventy-five years, Gary's agency offers services from over one hundred highly regarded insurers, covering homes, automobiles, and other personal and corporate needs.

Gary is lucky in that he stepped into a successful, well-established business. His clients are loyal, his vendor relationships are strong, and he has a trusted team of

---

37 www.BMRins.com

long-term members. However, luck alone doesn't keep a business moving forward.

When Gary and I began working together, I learned that he wanted to both expand his business and reduce his own hours to devote more time to his family.

In this regard, he'd already made great progress. Understanding that exceptional customer service had propelled the family business for generations, Gary implemented a robust customer service measurement system, affording every new customer the opportunity to provide feedback once their policy was in place.

Several of these forms came in every day, and Gary made it a point to review every single one. When one such survey response from a longtime customer indicated a less-than-ideal experience, Gary called the customer to apologize and ask what his company could do to improve things. The customer explained that everything had gone smooth enough, but that he wished he had received a renewal reminder a few weeks before the policy was up.

That sounded reasonable enough, but Gary knew his company already had alert systems in place to send renewal reminders. Certain there was more to the story, Gary checked the details on file for the customer and discovered they had his wife's contact information rather than his. One easy fix later, and now both husband and wife receive copies of all details and reminders.

NEVER SETTLE

Have you ever received negative feedback that surprised you? Did you start to wonder whether you were either viewing your team through rose-tinted glasses or being misled about the quality of the service you provide? If your processes are in place, and you have a staff you can trust, it could be that your customer wasn't a good fit with your company—or it could be that you've still got work to do.

In my coaching work, I've found there's only one type of business owner I can't work with, and it's those who are happy with the status quo.

It's not that I don't want to work with people who are content. However, I've found that I simply don't have much to offer someone who's not pushing to get better.

To work with me, a business owner must want to change or improve in some way—just like you. Seriously, pat yourself on the back for committing to your business by picking up or downloading this book. No doubt you've learned a few tricks that you're eager to try out, but before you do, here are some tips to help you put it all together.

ALL EYES ON THE CUSTOMER

To help them up their business game from good to great, I tell all my clients to be like Gary and focus on delivering outstanding customer service. However, this doesn't mean focusing on the customer. Rather, it means focusing on your team.

Why? The customer experience is inherently linked to the team member experience. Your team is on the front line, interacting with your customers, keeping your customers coming back, and making your company work. If they're happy, they'll work tirelessly to make your customers happy too.

Do you have a favorite coffee house, restaurant, or retail outlet? I bet you do, and I bet it's the people working there that keep you coming back. You may not know their names, but you'd recognize them and even make sure to greet them outside of the work environment if you happen upon them.

When it comes down to it, *Cheers* had it right. Sometimes you really do want to go where everybody knows your name. If you hire well, your outstanding customer service team will keep your customers coming back.

THE POWER OF FOUR

To recap, there are two major stakeholders for continual improvement: your customers and your team. Committing to continually improve requires us to think of these two stakeholders in two different ways—referrals and removals.

Referrals form the backbone of a concept called the Power of Four, so let's take a moment to explore the concept of referrals and discover why they're so valuable to business owners.

#1: ADDING CUSTOMERS: WHY REFERRALS MATTER

The easiest way to get new customers is through referrals. People prefer to do business with people they know or know of, so when a customer or team member introduces you to a prospect, that prospect is already much more comfortable than someone on the other end of a cold call. Few things reassure us like a positive endorsement from someone we trust.

While most business owners recognize the power and importance of referrals, they find those referrals hard to get. Usually, it's because they don't have a system in place to encourage referrals.

The Price of Losing Customers

If you don't have a system already, it's time to put one in place. There's no sense in losing otherwise happy customers—and failing to get new ones—purely due to negligence. Not only does it cost an average of five times more to get a new customer than it does to get repeat business from an existing one,[38] but losing clients has other negative impacts on your company:

- Lost sales and revenue
- Ability to pay suppliers or payroll
- Ability to grow the business
- Lost feedback and opportunity to improve
- Demoralization to you and your team
- Potentially negative word-of-mouth, which impacts your reputation among prospects, customers, suppliers, and your team
- Increased urgency to find new customers over nurturing existing ones
- Opportunities for your competitors to capitalize
- Distraction from other important issues

---

38 Amy Gallo, "The Value of Keeping the Right Customers," *Harvard Business Review* (October 29, 2014).

- Negative impacts to planning by damaging sales forecasts, cash flow, receivables, and payables
- Increased doubt about the validity of service fulfillment and pricing strategies
- Increased urgency to spend unbudgeted funds on marketing and new customer acquisition
- Disrupted inventory levels, investments, ordering processes, and reorder frequencies
- The potential for an accounting, legal, or collection nightmare
- Devaluation of the worth and salability of your company

Taking averages from a range of private studies tells us the following:

- 68 percent of customers leave because they feel poorly treated.[39]
- 95 percent of people who have had a bad experience don't complain to the business.[40]
- 13 percent of those who suffer a bad customer service experience tell twenty people, while satisfied customers only tell five.[41]

---

39 CSM: The Journal and Resource for Customer Service Managers and Professionals.

40 Customer Experience Impact 2010 Report.

41 White House Office of Consumer Affairs, Washington, D.C.

All this is to say that once you have customers, try not to lose them. The consequences are many, and the benefits are pretty slim.

Net Promoter Score

Who gives referrals? Your happiest customers.

Who are your happiest customers? To answer that, we have to figure out how to effectively measure customer satisfaction.

The Net Promoter Score (NPS) is still fairly new in business circles, but it's quickly gaining traction and has stacks of scientific research behind it. NPS was first developed and launched by Fred Reichheld in his 2003 *Harvard Business Review* article, and the concept immediately transformed the business world. Since then, businesses of all sizes have adopted it, from small start-ups to brands like Siemens, Philips, GE, Apple, American Express, and Intuit.

This revolutionary metric gauges customer experience and predicts business growth by providing core measurements for customer experience programs. The NPS ranges between -100 (everybody is a detractor) to +100 (everyone is a promoter). Any NPS greater than zero is considered good. If your score is above fifty, your business has an excellent reputation.

Your Net Promoter Score is determined by the answer to a single question: "How likely are you to recommend this company/product/service to a friend or colleague?" Responses are given on a scale of zero to ten. Scores of six or below are detractors, scores of seven and eight are neutral, and scores of nine and ten are promoters.

Once you have these responses, then take the following actions:

1. Add up the totals for each group.
2. Determine what percentage of the total number of respondents each group represents.
3. Subtract the percentage of detractors from the percentage of promoters.
4. Whatever number you're left with is your NPS.

Think of your initial score as a benchmark to improve on. For even better insights, give your customers a chance to elaborate. Along with their initial zero to ten rating, ask for an explanation. *Why* did they give you the score they did?

How and When You Implement NPS

Different business models will need to time their NPS surveys differently. Start by looking at all the customer touchpoints in your sales process. This could lead you down a couple different paths:

- **The sale-and-delivery approach.** If you sell products or services on a one-off basis, like a washing machine or a house painting service, your customer may not need to repurchase again for many years. In that case, send your NPS survey within a few days of delivery.
- **The repeat business approach.** Your timing here will depend on how often your customers need your service. My client Gary sends out an NPS every time a customer insures or renews. My client Ed the CPA sends out an NPS a few days after the end of tax season. Since my client Melissa has multiple customer touchpoints with the same small group every week, she sends out her surveys either once a quarter or annually.

Be sure to consider frequency as well. Your goal is to strike a balance between getting constructive feedback and hassling your customers. If someone purchases from you every week or two, don't constantly bombard them with NPS surveys. Think about what works for your business, and then put checks in place to avoid overloading your customers with requests.

Delivery matters too. While you could send your survey via snail mail, email is probably the safer bet in the digital age. It only takes a few minutes to set up and doesn't cost a penny. Digital surveys also make it easier for your customers to respond, which increases the likelihood they actually will. Store your responses electronically, and then measure and compare data at will.

How Does NPS Help Get Referrals?

With an NPS system in place, you'll always know who your happiest customers are. You will also know they'll respond positively and they're willing to interact with you if you reach out. Try something like this as your response:

> I'm so pleased you're happy with our work. Do you know anyone else who can benefit from our services?

Be specific when you're asking for referrals. If you're looking for high-net-worth prospects, mid-size companies, or small businesses, say so. If you're not specific regarding your needs, then your referrals won't be either.

To really boost your efforts, keep a list of the top twenty-five people or businesses you want to work with. That list may change over time, and you'll need to do some research to get it right, but asking for specific referrals off this list really does work. And it doesn't have to sound forced or awkward. Try this dialogue, for example:

> I'm so pleased you're happy with our work. Do you know anyone else who can benefit from our services? In fact, do you know Allison Miller at NettResults? No? No problem. NettResults is a great PR agency. Do you happen to know any other account directors at PR agencies?

While any kind of referral is great—even if it's just a name, email address, or phone number—the best kinds are those with the more personal touch. If your customer says they are happy to refer you to someone, ask for an introductory email or phone call, or invite both parties to lunch on your dime.

Once you're well-practiced and comfortable with this process, get a little more sophisticated and do deeper research before you ask for referrals. Use CRM systems and social media platforms like LinkedIn to establish who your customers are connected to, paying particular attention to any connections on your top twenty-five list. That way, you'll know exactly who to ask that promoter to refer you to.

Let's set a simple process for this:

1. Set a goal for the number of referrals you want to close.
2. Multiply that by your closing rate. That's the number of referrals you need to get.
3. Because not everyone will be compliant, you need to ask for twice the number of referrals you want to get.
4. Set a timeline and commit. Remember, calling brings you a far greater return rate than email does. Can you commit to calling ten promoters per week?

Here's another point to consider: referrals are high-value leads, so you need to work them quickly. In theory, this means you only want to work a handful at a time. Ask yourself, if you work at these referrals all day or all week and end up with ten hot leads all at once, can you really give each of them the attention and service they deserve? Be careful not to bite off more than you can chew.

Finally, remember to cultivate your existing business relationships by thanking the customer who referred you. Send them an email to let them know how you're getting on, or maybe send them a small gift as a token of your appreciation.

#2: ADDING TEAM MEMBERS: RECRUITING TALENT VIA REFERRAL

Asking team members for referrals is the most effective way of recruiting top talent. A CAP study published in *American Progress* found that the average hiring cost varies by wage and role.[42] The study showed that replacing a low-level team member earning under $30,000 costs 30 percent of their annual salary. Replacing a mid-level team member earning between $30,000 and $50,000 is 20 percent of their annual salary. Meanwhile, filling executive positions costs 213 percent of the exec's annual salary.

Regardless of the position or how you're recruiting, filling a vacancy takes time and money away that could be better spent elsewhere. Further, if you're like most business owners, you won't be able to resist the temptation of looking at applications as they hit your inbox, which is a major unproductive drain on your time.

I know what you're thinking. Wouldn't the process be much better if the best recruits just appeared, and you didn't have to spend time and budget on the process of attracting, sorting, and wooing them? After all, if it costs you 20 percent of a mid-level manager's $40,000 salary, that comes out to $8,000 just to hire someone. Yikes.

---

42 Heather Boushey and Sarah Jane Glynn, "There Are Significant Business Costs to Replacing Employees," *Center for American Progress* (November 16, 2012).

Team member referrals help you find better talent more quickly, meaning some of that $8,000 you'd normally spend on recruiting will instead go toward the first few months of your new manager's salary.

Fit is vital to the success of your team. Who hasn't wanted to make clones of their favorite team members? While you may not be able to do that, getting referrals from these top performers is the next best thing.

Back in 2011, *Scientific American* published a study titled, "Group Processes and Intergroup Relations." The study found that when asked to choose friends from a large, diverse pool, participants would pick those most similar to themselves. These findings align with the growing body of research that shows we humans have a universal preference for similarity, from our behavior to our initials.

This is good news for you. After all, if Bob is your ideal team member, and you wouldn't mind having a few more Bob-like team members around, just ask him. Odds are he'll know at least one or two other people with similar qualities (or at least similar initials).

PRO TIP

If you're directly responsible for recruiting, set up a separate email address for applications and commit to checking that email address once a day for a set maximum amount of time.

How Do You Get Your Team to Make Referrals?

Start by creating a formal referral process within your organization and then motivate your team to use it. Remember, to be an effective motivator, you need to understand what drives your team members. One great way to establish this is by using a personality assessment tool like DiSC. This system focuses on six core motivators, which include:

1. **Theoretical.** Accumulating knowledge, facts, and research.
2. **Utilitarian.** Using resources to gain maximum return on investment.
3. **Aesthetic.** Self-actualization through experiencing variety, beauty, harmony, and balance.
4. **Social.** Helping others and resolving hatred, conflict, and injustices.
5. **Individualistic.** Gaining power, advancing one's position, and having a leadership role.
6. **Traditional.** Following a defined process at work that provides the foundation for all decisions.

Here, we see that rewards are helpful but not essential in driving sales. In fact, only 11 percent of team members report they make referrals because of a bonus income. With the right referral program, some businesses have managed to achieve a rate of 70 percent of all hires from referrals, without offering any cash incentives.

So, if it's not about the money, what other strategies can you, the business owner, use?

The Team Wins

Winning is easy when your team has the best players. The more they refer others they know and trust, the more they help themselves out.

Recognition

Who doesn't like to be noticed for doing something good? Show your appreciation when a team member makes a successful referral. It doesn't have to be anything fancy. It could be a personalized note, a phone call from the boss, or a certificate. Each one works well.

Low-Cost Rewards

You don't have to spend a fortune on big-ticket referral rewards. Consider low-cost options that still express your thanks. Try family movie tickets or product samples. Alternatively, offer your team member preferred shift schedules, their pick of vacation days, or a reserved parking spot.

KPI Inclusion

Show that referring talent is a serious issue and include it as a team KPI. Everyone loves to achieve their KPIs.

Internal Marketing

Sometimes, all you need is a note on a communal bulletin board saying you have an opening and are encouraging your team to help. Then post your success stories.

Onboarding

If you've found a great hire, it makes sense to ask them if they have anyone they'd like to refer during their onboarding process.

Cash Rewards

Up to this point, the focus has been alternatives to financial incentive. That said, there's nothing wrong with it, provided you give it a little thought first.

If you were to offer cash rewards, how much should they be? Well, remember that bit about recruiting costs being directly related to salary range? Since you already know the target salary range, you can establish recruiting costs and work out how much the referral is worth to you.

Start on the low end. You can always increase, but you can never decrease. That said, my own experience has taught me that even high-value incentives have their limits. I've found that referral bonuses higher than $1,500 actually bring a lower return on investment.

Alternative Approaches

Finally, here are some other things to keep in mind with referrals:

- For team members not motivated by personal enrichment, offer to donate to a charity.
- For basic leads—for instance, when a team member offers up the name and contact info for someone they

know *of* rather than know personally—offer a smaller reward of fifty to a hundred dollars.

- Offer rewards to non-team members, such as vendors, partners, and others in your social networks. It may turn up some high-quality talent.

But enough talk about hiring and referrals. Let's move to the flipside of the Power of Four. How could the removal of customers and team members benefit your company?

#3: REMOVING CUSTOMERS AND PROBLEM CLIENTS

"Problem clients." These two words are guaranteed to elicit all kinds of stories from any group of business owners. I'm sure you have plenty of stories involving unreasonable requests, fistfuls of hair, and sleepless nights. We've all been there.

Most business leaders are reluctant to end poisonous customer relationships, because in spite of the issues, they *are* paying clients, after all. It's easy to rationalize keeping these clients around in the short term, but here's the truth: the longer they're around, the more you're cheating your business out of more valuable, rewarding clients.

It's time we talked about how to make room for your ideal clients.

How to Fire a Problem Client

Getting rid of problem clients is challenging and often emotionally charged. However, it's a crucial milestone in your business. Each time you move past a problem client, you learn more about your own deal-breakers and how to define your ideal clients. You'll never filter out every problem client, no matter how good your onboarding process is, but letting them go does get easier with experience.

In the following sections, we'll review how to fire problem clients the right way. Before we do, however, let's talk about the four main goals of every approach:

1. Plainly explain the situation.
2. Thank them for their business.
3. Be professional. You never know where you or the client will be in the future.
4. Set expectations for what happens next.

As you read these scripts, remember they are just guidelines to help you frame your conversations, which are best had in person or at least over the phone. Don't end a relationship by email.

Even if your customer is a never-ending source of grief, you don't need to tell them that. The following example is honest without being blunt.

> Dear Customer,
>
> After strategic analysis of our long-term goals, we are shifting our focus to only serve a specific subset of existing customers. We therefore regret to inform you that our team will no longer be able to work on your account, as of [date]. To help you explore other providers, we recommend [companies X, Y, and Z]. Thank you for your understanding. Below, you'll find the next steps you can expect from our team.

This script works because it positions you as making a business decision and sets clear expectations for moving forward, letting you sever the relationship cleanly and professionally.

It also lets you send your competition those less-than-ideal clients. It might seem counterintuitive to give your competition new clients, but in this case, you're not exactly doing them a favor. Most businesses don't have any processes in place for weeding out problem clients and will take on any new customer. Sending your rivals the time wasters, the obstructively difficult, the emotionally abusive, and the generally problematic customers will make you look professional while effectively tying up your rival's resources, leaving you free to take on better clientele.

It's Not You. It's Me

This one is common in relationships, but it works in business too.

> Dear Customer,
>
> It's been great working together, but due to unforeseen personal circumstances, I'm no longer able to assist you. While I realize this is short notice, I wanted to handle matters in the most professional manner, and I believe that some notice is better than none. To avoid interruption of service, please find another provider as soon as possible, and I'll do my best to ensure there are no issues during the transition. Thank you for your understanding and support. Below is a list of what to expect from me between now and then.

This is a good framework for small businesses or freelancers. You can be as vague or specific as you like, and you will still appear helpful by listing the next steps.

Direct and Professional

Sometimes, it's best not to sugarcoat things. The fact is, if you're seeing problems, your client probably is too. Bring this out into the open with communications like this:

> Dear Customer,
>
> Recently, I've noticed issues with our working relationship. As such, although it isn't easy to say, I think another company many be a better fit for your specific needs. As of [date], my company will no longer be able to assist you. Thank you for your understanding. Below is a list of the next steps you can expect from us.

This is a particularly effective way of professionally ending a relationship with an emotional or aggressive client, because it's short, direct, and naturally resistant to any pushback.

Dealing with Pushback

You will likely get feedback from your fired clients, regardless of which script you use. If you happen to get an aggressive or emotional response, be direct and polite in your response. Here's one example you can use:

Thank you for your feedback, but this decision is final. As mentioned before, here's a list of what to expect between now and [date].

Using this response finalizes the relationship firmly and professionally. Hopefully, you won't have to use it often, but with "those" kinds of clients (you know which ones I'm talking about), it's unavoidable.

#4: REMOVING TEAM MEMBERS

Getting rid of a team member is much harder than getting rid of a customer. During our peer review boards, we often discuss underperforming colleagues with a focus on whether they can be pulled back on track or whether they need to be let go.

Most leaders don't want to go down this path, because it can be costly and cause the team member emotional and financial difficulties. Plus, if you don't do it right, firing someone can open your business up to liability or lawsuits. Nobody likes that kind of risk, but you have to address it.

In this regard, first things first. Look up laws and regulations for terminating employment in your area. I've worked all over the world, and I can attest to the fact that employment laws differ wildly. If you need to terminate someone, you really need objective reasons. Regardless of the law, talk with your advisors or other business owners before proceeding.

Another benefit of the quarterly KPI system (see Chapter 10) is it gives you an objective measurement of whether a team member is performing to expectations. Act quickly when problems arise, communicating performance issues clearly and coaching your team member on how to improve.

Document, Document, Document

Record everything. Make it very clear to your team member that should they continue to underperform, you'll have no choice but to terminate their employment.

Good documenting begins with good planning. Ask yourself the following questions:

- Does the person facing termination perform an exclusive role or have knowledge that nobody else on the team knows?
- Does the person have keys or passwords?
- Can you outsource? Can other team members pick up the slack?
- Do you need to bring in outside talent?

- How else could your business suffer without this person?
- Will existing relationships with vendors or customers be jeopardized?

Letting someone go is rarely a clean break. However, the more angles you consider ahead of time, the better your business will rebound when you're forced to let a team member go.

Getting It Over With

If the team member continues to underperform, it's time to let them go. Make sure you have a place where you can speak openly, in confidence, and away from other team members. My office in Dubai had an open plan, so we used the coffee shop downstairs for informal meetings and the stairwell for confidential conversations. It may not have been glamorous, but it worked.

If necessary, ask a third party to attend the meeting. This could be another team member, your business coach, or an advisor. Third party or not, know what you're going to say beforehand and get to the point within the first thirty seconds. In fact, keep the conversation as brief as you can. There's no need to give more details than you need to. The team member already knows what's brought you to this juncture.

Start with, "I'm sorry, but I'm going to have to let you go," and then get the details out of the way:

- When does the termination take effect?
- Are there any severance payments, and if so, when will they be paid?
- Remind them of any legal agreements that remain in place after their termination. Have all those details written down, with one copy for you and another for the team member.
- Finally, remain professional and calm and thank them for their work.

The last part is especially important, as this is an emotional moment. The terminated team member may lose their cool, so be sure you keep yours.

Exit Interviews

A team member exit interview is not an attempt to reverse an individual's resignation. Instead, it's an opportunity to learn why people are resigning to reduce future turnover.

Why Team Members Leave

Team members usually give one or more of the following reasons for leaving:

- Lack of recognition
- Feeling underappreciated
- Poor supervision
- Personality conflicts
- Unhappiness with the boss
- Stressful differences between team members and supervisors
- Lack of opportunity for growth
- The desire for more money
- Unhappiness with perceived inequalities

Whatever the case, it's your job to find out why your team member left, as their feedback will give you invaluable insight into the inner workings of your business.

Structuring Your Exit Interview

Here are ten steps for conducting a successful exit interview:

1. Focus on good team members who resign. Losing troublesome team members is not cause for concern.
2. Have interviews conducted by someone other than the team member's direct supervisor, as that relationship can influence the interviewee's responses.
3. Explain the purpose of the interview to the attendee so they know they can speak freely.

4. Explain the confidential nature of the process and assure the person that their responses will be anonymous to anyone other than those in the interview.
5. Keep the interview simple and relatively brief.
6. Conduct the interview in private and preferably one-on-one.
7. Remember that not everyone is comfortable exploring the reasons they are leaving for fear of repercussions, such as poor future references.
8. Ask the team member to summarize their employment experience before asking specific questions. This usually answers some of the targeted questions before you ask them.
9. Assure the team member that no permanent record will be retained and that the notes will be discarded once assessed.
10. Assess and tabulate information gathered in exit interviews to help prevent further loss of good team members.

Above all, avoid being standoffish. This outgoing team member is doing your business a favor. Respect them and their time.

What to Ask

With the ground rules established, here are seven common exit interview questions to ask your outgoing team member:

1. How do you feel you were treated by your supervisor and coworkers?
2. How well do you believe your work was recognized and appreciated?
3. Do you feel you were given adequate training and assistance to perform your role?
4. Could you see opportunities for promotion or growth with this company?
5. How would you describe the morale of your fellow team members?
6. How fairly was the workload distributed?
7. What could be done to make this company a better place to work?

After that, ask if they have any further feedback that was not covered by your questions. Then, thank them for their time and service and wish them luck wherever they may land.

And that's the Power of Four—four ways to make your business better:

1. More customers through NPS and referrals
2. More team members through employee referral programs
3. Fewer customers through terminating poor customers and focusing on ideal customers
4. Fewer team members by focusing on the best people on your team

BACK TO ACADEMIA

Outside of my work commitments, I lecture at Chapman University. I do it not for the money, but because it's my chance to give back and scout new talent. I try and lecture in a fun, real-life way with passion and boldness to engage the students.

I started teaching purely by accident. One day at my home in Southern California, some new neighbors moved in next door to us and came over to introduce themselves. They explained they were the incoming chancellor and dean of a local university and apologized in advance for any parties that were a little too loud. They explained that because of their jobs, they had to entertain regularly, but we were welcome to come over and join in the festivities.

A few weeks later, we grabbed a couple bottles of wine and did just that. In the course of my conversation with this couple, two things came out: (1) I was a published coauthor of a previous book, and (2) I had a master's degree. Thrilled at this information, they asked me to teach a class. I was sold.

My classes focus on life after my students have completed their studies. Maybe they're moving on to another class, moving up in an existing job, pursuing the best job in their field, or embracing the concept of becoming entrepreneurial.

Whatever the case may be, at the end of every course, the university tracks how well the students did and how well the lecturer was received. The university team reviews multiple factors:

- Was the lecturer easy to understand?
- Did the lecturer provide solid feedback to the students?
- How well did the instructor provide course information?
- Did the instructor adequately describe how the class was evaluated?
- Did the instructor provide appropriate assignments?

Beyond these metrics, the university encourages students to leave personalized feedback about what they did and didn't like about the course.

When I go through this process, I encourage my students to give creative, honest responses, because I want to understand how to improve. In fact, I use my own NPS to determine how well I interact with my students.

I love getting this feedback. Not only do I use the metrics to plot the success of my course each semester, but I also playfully compete against the other professors to see who can get the most creative responses from students.

Some students eagerly go the extra mile, including pictures, sketches, and stories of how they will apply what they've learned to their daily lives. Some describe how some of the tools we use in the classroom are helping them to land their dream jobs. So, not only do these forms help improve our own processes, but they also help students focus on their own goals.

THE PASSION, PROFITABILITY, AND HAPPINESS INDEX

There isn't a normal route anymore. People go to college for all kinds of reasons. If they're in my class, I know I can help them get where they want to be—and satisfy my own passion, profitability, and happiness requirements in the process:

- **Passion.** I teach for the passion and opportunity to meet new people and potentially new talent. I lecture on strategic communication subjects, like marketing, advertising, and promotion, so it ensures I stay up-to-date with how students are using social media and interacting with brands.
- **Profitability.** I take many lessons from the interactions with my students and apply them directly to my own clients. I am also able to recruit new team members. Trust me, hand-selecting the best from a class of sixty qualified individuals is a big advantage.
- **Happiness.** I love learning from my students and sharing my own twenty-five-plus years of experience. It makes my job more fun and my life more rewarding.

Do you have any teaching or mentorship opportunities in your life? If not, I'd recommend it. Don't worry; you don't need a university job to make a difference. Look around. I'm sure you'll find plenty of opportunities.

FINAL TAKEAWAYS

I'm a big fan of fine-tuning. It means I've established a strong foundation for my business and things are running pretty smooth overall. Here are my three favorite approaches to perfecting my business:

1. The Net Promoter Score is a little piece of magic. Use it.
2. Your most important stakeholders are your customers and your team.
3. The two most important improvement factors are referrals and removals.

By now, you've got the basic tools you need to get yourself and your business exactly where you want to be. Lucky for you, we've got one more chapter to go. Are you ready?

NOW FOR SOME FUN

What's the best customer or team member referral you ever received? Have you been able to bottle that experience and make it a process?

Once you've given it some thought, share here:

http://exactlywhereyouwanttobe.com/poweroffour

CHAPTER 13

WHERE YOU WANT TO BE IS... ALWAYS MOVING

———

*The biggest risk is not taking any risks. In a world
that is changing really quickly, the only strategy
that is guaranteed to fail is not taking risks.*

—MARK ZUCKERBERG

Meet Michael Haag, owner of Productive Programming
Inc.,[43] a successful networking management solutions and
custom programming company founded in 1986. They
work on an array of productivity-minded programming
solutions, from automating processes to cost tracking.
They help businesses work smarter and increase efficiency.

43 www.propro.com

Michael's company also provides managed services, such as network monitoring and local and remote remediation.

When I first started working with Michael, he had a clear objective, which was to work on succession planning. He didn't want to sell his company. Instead, he wanted to let his team members take ownership while he took on a salaried role that didn't require him to be pulled into day-to-day management.

To this end, we worked on a variety of factors, including people, structures, and processes. At the beginning of one meeting, he told me that his wife of many years—a wonderful woman I'd met socially—was sick and in declining health. The couple faced some serious medical expenses, and understandably, Michael wanted to make his wife his first priority. He was even prepared to sell his business so he could support his wife financially.

In under an hour, we shifted the focus of our coaching session to the sale, profitability, goal-setting that was consistent with both his business and personal vision, and putting his succession plan on the back burner.

Within four months, Michael was seeing enough extra revenue from his company, which allowed him to take additional dividends and pay his wife's medical bills.

Better news still, just over nine months later, Michael's wife was on the road back to full health. In fact, as I write this, the couple has just returned from a celebratory trip to the Kentucky Derby, and Michael's succession plan is back in full swing.

TURN AND FACE THE CHANGES

Have you ever had external factors beyond your control force a quick change in your business? What would make you want to shift your goals? Are you confident enough in your vision and core values that you can make real changes?

No matter your plans, things change, and that's good. Embrace, adapt, and move forward. However, when you pivot—and it may need to happen quickly—make sure you hold tight to your personal and business visions and your core values.

Do you remember writing your personal and business visions way back in Chapters 2 and 3? Here is where it all pays off. In these moments of change, your vision and values help you quickly assess your needs and pivot to meet them.

No matter what, you'll be making a reactive move, but this way, you'll at least have a strong basis for whatever decisions you have to make. Besides, as long as you know who you are and what you stand for, reactive moves often pay off. For instance, some of the best businesses I work with reacted and downsized quickly enough in the face of the Great Recession of 2008 to keep their businesses alive to fight another day.

In fact, many businesses prospered. Unfortunately, those that didn't react fast enough weren't around to hire my services—or anyone's. Being reactive is easier than being proactive, and no matter what business you're in, you often have to react quickly in order to thrive.

Now for a little piece of magic, here's a simple formula that's sure to make your business better, regardless of the challenges you might face.

IDENTIFYING AREAS FOR IMPROVEMENT

Evolution is a natural part of being in business. The trick is knowing *how* you should evolve—and when. When it comes down to it, you need three elements working in sync to make the necessary improvements.

PROCESSES

I love having processes—and you should too. Remember, when you prepare to steer your company in a new direction, you must bravely lead the way so others will follow. But first, you must plot your course:

- **Results.** Clearly definite your desired outcome.
- **Documents.** Put everything you do in writing so team members can follow the process.
- **Tools.** The tools required for team members to complete the job can range from an adequate coffee machine to the right computer equipment and everything in between. Give them what they need.

Now that you know what you need to do, it's time to start walking the walk.

ACCOUNTABILITY

Your team members may be accountable to you, but who are you accountable to? In my work, I've learned that business owners are often far more effective when they're accountable to someone else. Make use of a neutral third party, such as a mentor, coach, or advisory board, to help you learn to lead more effectively.

For this to work, you need bidirectional trust to allow honest communication. Take the advice from your third party seriously, and use it to give your team the appropriate resources and training it needs to help you evolve your business. You're bound to have to delegate some tasks, so remember to follow up. This action step will ensure that quality standards, deadlines, and budget have been met.

MOTIVATION

The biggest challenge with taking your company in a new direction isn't deciding what to do, but convincing others to come with you. Communicate your business vision clearly to your team and instill in them your core company values. Let your team know why you're in business and what your cause is beyond money. If you need to, repeat the process at the individual level, focusing on your vision, values, and cause to connect the task to the person to whom it's assigned.

INTRODUCING THE PAM CYCLE

I take pride in being able to identify and offer solutions for any business area in need of improvement. Often, the big troubles I see have to do with stagnancy or complacency. If not, it's usually a breakdown in process, accountability, or motivation:

- A business with good processes and solid accountability, but lacking in motivation, is likely to come across as compliant and not fun at all.
- A business with good accountability and motivation, but lacking in good processes, often experiences erratic performance.
- A business with good processes and motivation, but lacking in accountability, will see its performance slowly decline. Everyone may be motivated to do a good job, but no one knows what a good job looks like.

To keep this from happening to your businesses, use the processes, accountability, and motivation (PAM) cycle. This will help you identify and solve any problem. The PAM cycle starts with two simple questions, which are:

1. Has the problem happened more than once? If not, ignore it in this context.
2. For repeat problems, define the result or change you want to see, and write it down. Keep it simple: "Instead of X, I want Y."

Next, we use the PAM cycle to identify the root of the problem.

PROCESSES

1. Do you have documented processes to deal with the problem?
2. Are the processes accurate and relevant?
3. Has responsibility been clearly defined?
4. Does your team have the tools it needs to be successful?

ACCOUNTABILITY

1. Are results measurable and measured?
2. Can desired actions or behaviors be improved through training?
3. How consistent and effective is your follow-up?
4. Are one-on-one meetings being held when necessary?
5. Does your team trust its managers?

MOTIVATION

1. Is your team member motivated to work at your company?
2. Are your company values clearly defined?
3. Does your team believe in your company values?
4. Do your team members have visions for their career?

PUTTING PAM TOGETHER

By answering these questions, you can easily identify where your problems are and how you can improve them. Create a new process explaining what you plan to do, when, and how.

That's the PAM cycle. It's exceptionally simple and effective. In fact, I use the PAM cycle at least once a week when I am coaching business owners. Usually, after a general conversation with a prospect I've never met before, I can identify whether the problems at their company stem from a process, accountability, or a motivational issue.

MAKING CHANGES PROACTIVELY

While it's true that reactive changes made within the right framework can benefit your business, wouldn't you rather be the one driving the change rather than responding to it?

That's what proactive change is all about—and it's something I would recommend doing at the end of every financial year. To help you in this quest, here's a list of seven annual statements for your consideration that are designed to keep you in the driver's seat:

1. Last year, our revenue was $X. This coming year, we expect our revenue to be $Y. This is an increase or decrease of $Z.
2. The one thing that will most significantly hinder our ability to do this is _____.
3. Our profit margin (or gross net) will go from X percentage to Y percentage.
4. The biggest improvement we can make to increase profit in the next twelve months is _____.
5. By the end of the year, my personal role within the company will have changed in the following manner: _____.
6. To accomplish my role change, I need to _____.
7. This year, my company's ability to provide the quality of life I seek will be indicated by my ability to meet my goals on a personal scorecard that I will provide.

With regards to your scorecard, make sure you set measurable goals, such as the number of nights you are home on time, the number of rounds of golf you will play in a month, or the weeks of vacation you plan to take over a year.

BONUS QUESTIONS

Want a little more value? Here are four more questions to help you get started.

1. What part of your business needs the most improvement?

2. What could you do to have the most impact on your business?

3. What major effort will take close to a year to accomplish?

4. Which projects and actions must be completed in order to accomplish the others?

These questions will help you identify any number of areas within your business that you may need to improve, revamp, or replace. These include training, market research, bidding processes, policies, procedures, computer software, team members, value-added services, infrastructure investments, marketing programs, strategic planning, organizational structure, turnaround times, cost of goods sold, customer satisfaction, purchase or cost controls, accounting systems, or cash flow funding. You name it, and it helps.

DASHBOARDS

Say I offered you a pair of trendy eyeglasses. What if I told you when you put them on, you would have a clear, unbiased view of how your business was performing and where you should put your own focus? Would you want them?

Well, with a good dashboarding process, that's exactly what you get.

"GOOD ENOUGH" ISN'T GOOD ENOUGH

While the tools already exist to give you unprecedented visibility into your business, many business owners tell me they're not interested in my magic glasses. They say that whatever systems they currently have are good enough.

However, when I press them for more information, I start to get a different picture. They may think they have an idea of how things are going, but it's only an approximation. The data is often scattered and incomplete.

This can lead to some awkward conversations. When I meet a business owner for the first time, I am hesitant to ask about their revenue, profit, or cash flow. It's not that they're afraid to talk about such things. Rather, they're embarrassed by their own lack of knowledge and inability to access the information.

WHY DASHBOARDS?

As embarrassed as these business owners might feel, they're not alone. I've found that very few businesses have real-time data at their fingertips. And that's why very few businesses are truly successful in the long-term.

What gets measured gets done. Accurate, real-time metrics and reporting keeps you focused, allows you to make better decisions, and improves your results. If this sounds like solid business sense to you, then it's time you invest in a dashboard.

The term *dashboard* applies to any system, usually online, that tracks sales, cost of goods sold, accountability, and an array of other metrics, and then presents that data in an accessible, easy-to-understand display. They're powerful tools, and all the most successful people I work with use them to view critical success factors and track KPI progress in real time.

THE DIFFERENCE BETWEEN METRICS AND MEASURES

Before we get too far into how dashboards work, let's get some definitions of measures and metrics straight:

- A **measure** is a quantitative number that counts something (e.g., we made $10,000 profit last month).
- A **metric** gives you more information by comparing the measure to a baseline (e.g., we made $10,000

profit last month, $3,000 more than the same month last year).

In other words, a measure is merely a number, but a metric gives that number valuable context.

LAG AND LEAD METRICS

A lag metric tells you the result of something. We call it a lag metric because it lags behind the time for action: once you have the information, that's it. For instance, we made $10,000 profit last month, which is $3,000 more than the same month last year. That's that; there's nothing more to see here.

Lag metrics are helpful, but a good business owner like yourself wants to be more *proactive* than *reactive*, right? That's where lead metrics come in. Lead metrics help you track the KPIs most likely to impact your bottom line before you measure the bottom line. For instance, one lead metric could be that your business has averaged five sales calls per week for the last three weeks, putting you above your target of three calls per week.

WHAT SHOULD BE MEASURED?

I've run the following exercise with many different businesses, and the results never look the same. Inevitably, different businesses need different measures and metrics, and therefore, different dashboards.

That said, I can suggest a few things for you to look at. For starters, try breaking your data down into the following three areas:

Strategic Dashboards

These track the key performance indicators of your business. The data behind a strategic dashboard updates on a recurring basis. For example, your strategic dashboard could provide visualizations of financial, operational, sales/marketing, and customer experience data at a company level. Update and view these dashboards daily to stay on top of the KPIs that matter most.

Analytical Dashboards

An analytical dashboard is used to analyze large volumes of data to allow you to investigate trends, predict outcomes, and discover insights. The data behind an analytical dashboard needs to be accurate and up-to-date.

Analytical dashboards often include advanced business intelligence features, like drill-down and ad hoc querying. For example, an analytical dashboard could help you view multiple metrics on each sales agent, including the number of calls made, quotes provided, average time to close a sale, number of sales, average revenue per sale, and the customer satisfaction score. Think of all the fun you could have with that data!

Operational Dashboards

Want to know what's happening in your business right now? An operational dashboard monitors business processes that frequently change, and it tracks the current performance of key metrics. For example, your operational dashboard may track hourly web performance against predetermined objectives for your digital marketing team.

This kind of data updates very frequently, sometimes even on a minute-by-minute basis. Therefore, you may need to monitor this dashboard multiple times daily.

WHAT'S ON YOUR DASHBOARD?

Not sure what to put on your dashboard?

Your business vision from Chapter 3 makes a great starting point. If you know where you want to be and you also know what is critical for your success, then you probably already have some goals in place.

From there, look at measures and metrics that pertain to the whole business. Ask yourself these questions:

- What data do I have right now, and where can I find it?
- What data do I not have, and what would I like to have? How can I rectify that?
- To reach my business goals, what do I need to know?
- If I had real-time, accurate data, what would I do with it?
- Where are we flying blind?
- What do I want to know each day that I usually reach out to coworkers to learn?
- When I access systems today, what do I look at most?
- What could I have improved or prevented in the last year with an advance warning?

Get the idea? These questions aren't meant to be exhaustive, but they should get you thinking. At this stage, I encourage you to brainstorm as many different measures and metrics as you can. It's easy to remove the useless or redundant stuff afterward.

LOGISTICS

Now that you know what data you want, how do you get it all in one place to create a snapshot of your business?

There are plenty of dashboard programs out there, but if I'm being honest, you may find the available options lacking. In true entrepreneurial spirit, many of my clients have hired freelancers or consultants to build specific dashboards to suit their needs. This may cost more up-front, but ultimately, it leads to better business results.

MEASURING SUCCESS

Speaking of better business results, how do you measure the success of your new dashboard system? The easiest measure is adoption. If you, the forward-thinking business owner, really do look at your dashboard and learn something new at least once a day, then you have a successful dashboard.

Will your dashboard need to be updated as your business grows? Absolutely. As your needs and knowledge change, so should your dashboard. However, success ultimately depends not on how often you have to update, but rather on how seriously you take the project and how committed you are to using the tools you've put in place.

BONUS DASHBOARDING TIP

If you want to become a dashboard superstar, this last bit is for you. If you can achieve it, I would love to speak to you, since I consider this tip the holy grail of management for a medium-size company.

We've talked about how to manage your team and the importance of KPIs. Further, we've talked about how your dashboard can measure your business's KPIs.

Knowing that, wouldn't it be great if you could drill down from your company dashboard and see the real-time KPIs of each department and team member in your organization?

How would that make you feel? Would you be able to sleep better at night? Would you be able to take more time off work? Would you feel like a lighter, better version of yourself and actually commit to spending more time on making your business better?

I think you would, but the question is: How do you make that a reality?

If you figure it out, let me know. I would love to see how you engineered those eyeglasses.

BUSINESS REVIEWS

Before I wrap up this chapter and send you on your way, let's talk about one last thing: business reviews. These reviews are great for checking in not only on where you've been, but also on where you're going.

Thankfully, there's a simple process to follow here. Begin by identifying two to four factors that most positively impacted your business, and then do the same for the factors that most negatively impacted it.

From there, I've outlined the following seven areas for you to cover. For each one, list up to three things you need to start, stop, and continue doing to drive your business forward:

1. Marketing and sales
2. Business operations
3. Product service offerings
4. People and culture
5. Customer service
6. Financial management
7. Your role as business owner

Most of us rarely sit down and examine our business in this way. Think about it: When was the last time *you* sat down and asked yourself what your business should stop doing? This process gives us valuable insights and lets us focus on important issues without becoming a huge drain on our time or resources.

Further, while it's true great business leaders aren't quitters, they may have processes that are either obsolete or ineffective. In my experience, I've learned that identifying what you need to stop doing is arguably more important than identifying things you need to start or continue doing.

That said, for the most comprehensive overview of the health of your business, make sure to list all three elements—things to stop, start, *and* continue—for each of the preceding seven points.

IN SEARCH OF THE NEXT STORY

After selling one of my businesses in the Middle East, my wife and I were left wondering what to do with the cash injection and extra time the sale afforded us. We considered investing the money into one of our other two businesses, but both were doing well already and didn't need the extra resources.

We decided it was time for something new. To make sure we started off on the right foot, first we reevaluated our personal and business visions, making sure not to compromise our existing values. For me, having served on so many advisory boards and groups, and having helped business owners work through their visions and overcome challenges, I had come to understand how lonely it can be at the top. Most business owners don't have anyone to speak to because they can't share many aspects of their business with others.

With this in mind, my wife and I decided that a peer advisory service made sense and fit well with our existing businesses. This business would match our passion, belief, and core values. If small businesses truly drive success in society, we would help drive success in small businesses.

By this time, we'd already seen plenty of success stories—small businesses that went from employing one or two people to providing hundreds of jobs, all while watching their revenues skyrocket from a few million to over $100 million. We'd witnessed firsthand the positive effects these businesses had on society and knew our new company could help other businesses eager to make an impact.

We began working with business owners both on a one-to-one coaching basis and in group settings to enable networking and collaboration, and things grew from there. Today, I'm proud to say it's one of the most fulfilling journeys I've undertaken. It's so powerful to meet a business owner twice a month, to watch them move closer to achieving their goals, and to help them attain their visions for themselves, their families, and their teams.

WRAPPING UP

I hope some of the stories, strategies, and lessons we've explored in this book will inspire the trailblazers and small- and medium-business owners across the globe.

We've established the importance of doing what you love in your business. Now it's time to ask yourself: *are* you? Is your business doing what you want it to? Does it allow you to have passion, profit, and happiness, or are you just doing what you're doing because you fell into it? Are you living to work or working to live?

When I first started NettResults in Dubai, our goal was to offer business plans and business setup services during the dot-com bubble. People were lining up to get their businesses off the ground.

However, while this was good for us, it also presented a challenge. Our service was positioned right at the start of the entrepreneurial life cycle, and many businesses simply didn't make it. We believed in what we were doing, but sometimes it felt like we weren't making a difference. We decided to adapt and began offering marketing and public relations services in the Middle East for a different, more established customer base, and soon, we were making a big difference to a lot of people.

With that, here's my final lesson for you: make your business what you want it to be.

As you're reading this, new businesses and opportunities are popping up all around us. You've heard many success stories in this book, but no doubt there are countless others. Each of these businesses has adapted because visionary owners went forth with a plan that would ensure they were where they wanted to be—all because their business was what they wanted it to be.

Now it's your turn. What do *you* want your business to be?

CHAPTER 14

THE FINAL SEND-OFF

———

*"So would you tell me please which
way I ought to go from here?"
"That depends a good deal on where
you want to get to," said the Cat.
"I don't much care where," said Alice.
"Then it doesn't matter which
way you go," said the Cat.
"So long as I get somewhere," Alice
added as an explanation.
"Oh, you're sure to do that," said the
Cat, "if you only walk long enough."*

—LEWIS CARROLL, ALICE IN WONDERLAND

Which path do you want to follow? You control your
destination.

The tools in the first part of this book have given you everything you need for your journey, while the rest of the book helped you develop specific, time-tested strategies for improving operations.

Will you come across problems and challenges along the way? Sure, you will. Running a business isn't easy. If it were, everyone would be doing it.

SEEKING THE CHAMPAGNE MOMENT

Before we go, I want to share a technique with you that I use every year with my clients. I call this the "champagne moment," that point when you've achieved what you've set out to do, and all that's left is to celebrate.

To create your own champagne moment, answer one question: What is the *one thing* you want to accomplish this year? Answer this question after you've completed your annual review, and it should be self-evident.

Let's revisit some of the leaders we met earlier and celebrate their champagne moments with them.

GEORGE

George's champagne moment is to build his retirement home in Croatia, and he's just approved the architectural design. He'll be in Croatia in a few months to oversee the start of the construction.

MELISSA

Melissa plans to add a video service to her marketing agency and complete three successful projects. When we last spoke, she was about to launch the new service on her website, already had a contract in-hand for the first project, and had at least three other parties interested in the new service.

TORREY

Torrey wants his video projects service to go from signed contracts to final edits without him having to get directly involved. He has worked hard to put detailed processes in place for his team, so he can be more hands-off with his latest projects. Now that that's in place, he's able to leave for a fun week in San Juan, Puerto Rico, on vacation with his wife, secure in the knowledge his customers are being looked after.

BRIAN

Brian's champagne moment is to write his book on customer service based on his experience in the bug industry. For this to become a reality, he needs to improve visibility for his executive team, increase sustainable and predictable cash flow, and work fewer hours in the business (so he can write). In the past five months, Brian has made huge progress in each of these areas.

CRYSTAL

Crystal is striving to achieve a net worth of $1 million and $5 million under management within her business. She's successfully outsourced all of her back-office work and has a team dedicated to applying her new sales strategy. She's on target.

STEVE

Steve's champagne moment is to pay dividends to his shareholders this year and to pay off their principle investment by next year. He's got a solid financial plan in place, and he's on target.

GARY

Gary is in the process of writing 600 new policies this year, has implemented a new sales strategy, and is on target to exceed his goal weeks before the end of the year.

MICHAEL

Michael is searching for a general manager to oversee the day-to-day operations of his business. He returned from a bucket list trip last month and has a strong team in place to help him achieve his champagne moment.

WHAT'S YOUR CHAMPAGNE MOMENT?

These business leaders all took steps to plan and execute with accountability, and as a result, they're all making great strides toward achieving their personal goals. You took the first step by picking up this book and reading it. Don't let it end there. Don't go back to the drudgery. Plan and execute your ideal business.

Start by setting your personal and business visions. What are your critical success factors? How are you going to proactively move your business forward? What is this year's champagne moment? Mine was writing this book.

Share yours here:

http://exactlywhereyouwanttobe.com/champagnemoment

Your next story hasn't been written yet, but make no mistake, you'll be the one to write it as you set forth on your next great adventure. You never know, maybe someone you meet tomorrow will change your course in an exciting new direction.

Exactly Where You Want to Be: A Business Owner's Guide to Passion, Profit, and Happiness isn't just a title. It's a linear plan for success. Building a business based on your passion will lead you to profit, and profit leads to happiness.

Be exactly where you want to be. Keep setting your destination and enjoy the trip.

DON'T BE A STRANGER!

What is your personal business vision? My business vision is to continually work with business owners across the globe and be a part of their success story. If you know a business owner who wants to take their operation to the next level, I want to know them.

Find out more here:

http://exactlywhereyouwanttobe.com

ABOUT THE AUTHOR

NICK LEIGHTON has spent more than twenty years working with entrepreneurs and business owners to take their personal and professional lives to the next level. Driving this work is a single vision: business owners should make more money and have more free time to achieve their life goals—whether that goal is writing more, partying at the Playboy Mansion, attending concerts, or living it up at Disneyland. After all, the more we love our lives, the more we love our work.

Made in the USA
San Bernardino, CA
23 January 2019